Dynamic Cover Letters

Dynamic Cover Letters

revised

*How to sell yourself
to an employer
by writing a letter that will get
your resume read, get you an interview,
and get you the job!*

Katharine Hansen
and
Randall S. Hansen, Ph.D.

TEN SPEED PRESS
Berkeley, California

TEN SPEED PRESS
Box 7123
Berkeley, California 94707

Cover design by Fifth Street Design
Text design by Paula Morrison
Illustration on page 61 by Akiko Shurtleff

Library of Congress Cataloging-in-Publication Data
Hansen, Katharine.
 Dynamic cover letters : how to sell yourself to an employer by
writing a letter that will get your resume read, get you an
interview, and get you the job! / Katharine Hansen and Randall S.
Hansen. — 2nd ed.
  p. cm.
 Includes bibliographical references.
 ISBN 0-89815-675-0 : $7.95
 1. Cover letters. 2. Résumés (Employment) I. Hansen, Randall S.
II. Title.
HF5383.H28 1995
650.14—dc20   94-46692
                                                CIP

Printed in Canada

1 2 3 4 5 6 7 8 9 10 — 99 98 97 96 95

To Three Special Men:

William Dayton Sumner

John N. Sumner

David L. Rhody

The authors wish to thank the following job-seekers who submitted cover letters for critiquing, thereby providing invaluable research for this book and models for many of the sample cover letters: Balan Dinesh, Boris Ivanov, Susan Cottingham, Satya Bhamidapati, B. Madhavan, John Smith, Jim Chapman, Isabel Lopez, Sundar Hariharan, Paul Kolenda, Joseph Pescatello, Roy Taylor, Nell Nguyen, Karthik Vasudevan, Lorena Peer, Daniel Clark, Mark Shaw, Nora Khammash, Adriane Moser, Dietmar Tietz, Jane Will, Krystan Douglas, William Sier, Elizabeth Sumner, Suzanne Kerigan, Chad Bleuel, Tricia Koen, Kim Aldrich, Tiffany Trenkle, Juliet Knauth, Holly Davis, Gretchen Flint, Ashleigh Scudder, Alisa Wagley, Abby Hodge, Lisa Long, Mary Fiester, Amy Koss, Karen Doyle, Gary Siebold, Francesco Fiondella, Dikran Toroser, Peace Wang, Konrad Kim, Michael Smith, Weni Ni, and Donna Hefner. The authors also thank Larry Line for his suggestions about the Internet.

For information on having your cover letter critiqued, write or e-mail:

Katharine and Randall Hansen
1250 Valley View Lane
DeLand, FL 32720-2364
khansen@suvax1.stetson.edu
hansen@suvax1.stetson.edu

Contents

Introduction to the Second Edition

YOUR COVER LETTER is the first thing an employer sees when you send out your resume. Experts on job-hunting say the purpose of a resume is not to get you a job, but to get you an interview. But the only way you're going to get an interview is if your resume is read.

The best way to ensure it will be read is to write a dynamic cover letter that will arouse the potential employer's interest. This book shows you how to write a dynamic cover letter.

What qualifies us to write about cover letters? After all, we're not career counselors. Some of our training has come from the trenches of job-hunting. We've used cover letters successfully in a number of job searches.

We've also been in the position to hire employees. Hundreds of cover letters—from terrific to atrocious—have come across our desks (and many of them, with name and other identifying features changed to protect privacy, appear in the sample section of this book). We speak from an employer's perspective; we know what turns employers on and what makes them toss your letter right into the circular file.

We've worked with college students and critiqued countless cover letters and resumes for them.

We're also writers who can apply our craft to the art of writing dynamic cover letters. With this book, we'll help you to write dynamic cover letters that will prompt employers to call you for interviews.

In the five years since our first edition appeared, the job market has become increasingly competitive. Downsizing has become the business buzzword of the 1990s. Companies are trying to do more with less—and with fewer employees. Recent college graduates are finding it harder than ever to land good jobs and are even voicing some concern that a college degree isn't worth much these days.

Even when the market was less cutthroat than it is now, as we approach the twenty-first century, experts claimed that only 1 in 245 resumes resulted in an interview. Given that statistic on top of current market trends, the job-seeker needs every competitive edge. A well-crafted, attention-getting, assertive cover letter can provide that edge. This new, expanded edition of *Dynamic Cover Letters* shows you even more ways to write a winning letter. We offer seventy-five effective cover-letter samples, virtually all of them new to this edition. We've beefed up the section on editing your letter and provided three cover-letter make-overs that show how to address specific problems with your letter.

We've added the "Cover Letter Hall of Shame" to show you how *not* to write your cover letter. And because more than ever you need to understand the job-hunting process, we've also added "The Big Picture" to give you a quick overview of everything you need to know in order to market yourself.

Another change since this book was first published has been the phenomenal growth of technology, and the advent of the information superhighway. Computer networks and other technological advances mean that not only are there new ways to transmit your job-hunting correspondence, but also vast new electronic avenues for discovering job openings.

This new edition offers numerous examples of letters to be sent over computer networks and explains how to use the information superhighway to uncover job leads.

We wish you much success—in using this book to develop *your* dynamic cover letters and in your job search.

—Katharine Hansen and Randall S. Hansen, Ph.D.

Send Not Thy Resume Naked into the World

WHAT IS A cover letter? Also known as a letter of introduction, letter of application, transmittal letter, or broadcast letter, it's a letter that no smart job-seeker should send his or her resume without. Few employers seriously consider a resume that is not accompanied by a cover letter. I know I didn't when I was in a hiring position.

Why is a cover letter so important? A resume is useless to an employer if he or she doesn't know what kind of work you want to do. A cover letter tells the employer the type of position you're seeking.

A dynamic cover letter can give you an edge in the competitive world of job-hunting. The experts say that only two to five of every hundred resumes survive the screening process. Clearly, you can increase your chances of being invited for an interview by writing an effective cover letter.

This is especially true because few applicants give much thought to their cover letters, even though they have put blood, sweat, and tears into their resumes. As the applicant who has taken pains to write a striking letter, you will stand out.

The cover letter is particularly useful if you don't have much relevant experience to put into a resume. It takes a lot less effort to write a cover letter that demonstrates you're the right person for the job despite your lack of experience than it does to actually obtain enough experience to beef up a skimpy resume.

A cover letter highlights the aspects of your experience that are most useful to the potential employer, and you can earn points for knowing what those aspects are. Employers get hundreds of resumes, especially when they advertise a choice position. Employers are also very busy. Often the person screening resumes scans each for only a few seconds. Your cover letter can call attention to the skills, talents, and experience the employer is looking for.

Your cover letter provides the opportunity to show what you know about the field you're interested in and the company you're writing to, as well as your written communication skills. Although some positions put a higher premium on writing skills than others, there are few positions in which the ability to write clearly is not an asset. A well-constructed cover letter can also demonstrate your ability to organize your thoughts and get to the point.

Your letter can explain things that your resume can't. If there are large gaps in your employment history or you are reentering the job market or changing

the focus of your career, a cover letter can explain these circumstances in a positive way.

A cover letter can serve the same function as the "job objective" on your resume, and expand upon it. Some applicants are reluctant to limit themselves by putting an objective on their resume. Although it is best for a job-seeker to target the type of work desired as specifically as possible, you may be open to more than one option. Instead of using only one objective on your resume—which you are not likely to tailor to each individual employer—you can vary your objective by the way you express it in your cover letter.

Finally, a cover letter is a little window into your personality. A good cover letter can suggest to an employer, "I'd like to interview this person; they sound like someone I'd like to get to know better. This seems like just the kind of dynamic person this company needs."

A cover letter is perhaps the most important part of a direct-mail sales package. The product is you. As with any other sales letter, you are trying to motivate a specific action. You want that employer to call and invite you for an interview. A dynamic cover letter can arrest the employer's attention and arouse their interest.

Three Kinds of Cover Letters

THERE ARE ROUGHLY three kinds of cover letters, each corresponding to a different method of job-hunting. Most successful job-seekers will find that they do not employ any one method or use any one kind of cover letter, but rather a combination of all three. To understand the three kinds of cover letters, it is helpful to look at these three types of job searches.

Only about one-fifth of the job market is what we call "open." That means that only about 20 percent of job openings are ever publicly known. The main avenue for informing the public about these openings is through want ads in the newspaper, trade magazines, and other publications. Employment agencies and executive-search firms are another source of open-market positions. The first kind of cover letter is the invited letter, which is generally a response to a want ad.

The other fourth-fifths of the market is "closed," meaning you can't find out about the positions unless you dig. That digging most often takes the form of compiling a list of all the companies in your field that you might be interested in working for and contacting them to ask for an interview. Obviously, that means some job-seekers will send out a great many resumes, accompanied

by the type of cover letter that we call the uninvited or cold-contact letter, sometimes blanketing a given field of companies with direct-mail packages.

The successful job-hunter will be persistent in following up on the interviews he or she asks for, even when the employer says there are no openings. Will the employer be annoyed with you for persisting in seeking an interview? Probably not—employers admire drive and ambition. Your persistence means you truly want to work for that company. When we were hiring, the "squeaky wheel gets the grease" approach worked on us almost every time.

A job-hunter who can get a few minutes of an employer's time can succeed in a number of ways. By finding out more about the company's needs, you may be able to create a position for yourself even though the employer has said no openings exist. More likely, however, you will learn a little more about your field, knowledge that you can apply to your job search.

Best of all, you can close the interview by saying, "I'm sorry to hear you have no openings, but perhaps you could suggest someone else in the field who does." If you've made a good impression in your interview, chances are the employer will give you not just one but several referrals.

And that leads us to the third kind of cover letter, a very close cousin to the uninvited letter. This letter, too, is uninvited but it has an edge. It prominently displays the name of a person your addressee knows. We call this kind of cover letter the referral letter. Referral letters are the product of networking, which many experts say is the most effective method of job-hunting.

A referral letter will start out, for example, "John Ross of Technology Unlimited suggested you might have openings for systems analysts."

Referral letters can come about from a number of different sources. You might talk with someone at a meeting of a trade association in your field who will tell you of an opening she knows of. An acquaintance at a party might tell you of someone he knows whose company could use an employee with your experience. A friend might tell you about a job she saw through her company's internal job-posting.

The method of job-hunting you choose will depend a great deal on your situation. If you already have a job and are interested in moving on but not desperate to get a new job, you may be content to read the help-wanted ads in your Sunday newspaper and respond to those that appeal to you.

If, however, you are mounting a major job search or are a recent graduate, you will probably conduct a more aggressive mass-mailing campaign, as well as monitoring the want ads closely and networking to seek contacts who can refer you to where the openings might be.

Next, we'll look at some of the characteristics peculiar to each kind of cover letter.

The Uninvited or Cold-Contact Cover Letter

THE UNINVITED LETTER is the most straightforward and has several advantages. (It enables you to use the exact name of the person who has the power to give you a job, if you can manage to find it out.) This is a key point. Whenever possible, any cover letter should be sent to a named individual. The largest employer in Central Florida, for instance, throws away any letter that does not address him by name. If you want to get an interview and hence a job, you can forget about using such salutations as "Dear Sir or Madam," "Gentlemen," "Dear Personnel Director," or "To Whom it May Concern." Those salutations tell the employer that you were not concerned enough to find out whom it concerns. We'll talk later about how to find out the name of the best person to address.

The uninvited cover letter provides an opportunity to show what you know about the company you're writing to. Demonstrating that you've done your homework is a good way to get a real edge on your competition. How many times, after all, have you been asked during an interview, "What do you know about our company?" Many employers use your knowledge of the company as a litmus test.

The uninvited cover letter enables you to take a proactive approach to job-hunting instead of the reactive approach, in which you merely answer ads. It can be a great tool for uncovering hidden jobs where supposedly no openings exist. Your letter can make such an impression that you'll be remembered as soon as there is an opening. You may also be able to create an opening for yourself by convincing the employer that they need someone with your talents. At the very least, you may obtain an interview in which the employer can refer you to others in the field who might have use for you.

The biggest disadvantage of the uninvited cover letter is that it is, after all, uninvited. When an employer doesn't have a current opening and hasn't solicited your letter and resume, he or she is likely to give it much less attention than if there had been an advertised opening. You can minimize this disadvantage by writing a letter that lets the employer know that you are someone he or she should pay attention to.

A key aspect of a successful direct-mail campaign with this letter is compiling a large list of potential employers—perhaps as many as several hundred. You must also research each company, to individualize your letters. We won't deal too extensively here with list compilation and research since our main focus is cover letters. A number of good books, however, offer general job-hunting techniques and deal extensively with developing job leads and researching potential employers. Several of these books are cited in Recommended Reading, page 143. You'll also find a list of sources for job leads on page 64.

The Invited Cover Letter

A COVER LETTER THAT is invited through a want ad offers the primary advantage that the employer expects and welcomes it; he or she has an opening, may be very anxious to fill it, and is hoping you will be the right person.

The invited cover letter also enables you to speak to the requirements of the ad. You can offer the employer the requirements sought because you *know* the requirements sought; it's all spelled out in the ad.

Whether or not you can write to a specific individual and demonstrate your knowledge of the company the same way you can with the uninvited letter depends on which ... you are responding to.

Many want ... mpany that placed the ad. When you know wha ... to, you can use the same strategies as with the ... arch the company and demonstrate your kno ... find out the best person to write to—unless the ... mpany wants you to write to.

Sometimes ... place blind ads, which do not identify the co ... panies place these ads because they don't wan ... y are trying to fill a position, or becaus ... want the obligation of responding to ...

Some blind ... ome use initials for the company name. So ... ce box. In these cases, it may still be possible to find ... dvertising. If you can do so, you can demonstrate your knowledge of the company, and the employer will most likely be impressed with your resourcefulness in identifying the company.

In her book *Put Your Degree To Work,* Marcia Fox tells a story about an ad that referred applicants to a "J. M. Smith." Only 1 of 300 respondents bothered to call the company and ask the full name of "J. M. Smith." Janet M. Smith appreciated the single letter addressed to her and was impressed with the motivation of the job-seeker who had gone to the trouble to learn her name. That job-seeker was also one of only three people interviewed for the position. The same applies when the ad asks you to write to "Personnel Director." If you know the name of the company, find out who the personnel director is.

The blindest of blind ads gives only a box number at the newspaper carrying the advertisement. The employer rents a box at the newspaper and uses it as an address to which applicants should respond. There is virtually no way to find out what company is advertising. Thus, you can't address your

letter to a named individual, and you can't talk about your knowledge of the company.

To whom should you address your letter when you don't know who the advertiser is? As mentioned earlier, avoid "To Whom it May Concern." "Gentlemen" is sexist. "Dear Sir or Madam" is acceptable, if a bit stilted and old-fashioned. I have often used "Dear Friends" as a cordial, non-sexist salutation, although some career experts have said it is too informal. Our current favorite for blind-box-ads is "Dear Boxholder."

It is also acceptable when responding to a blind-box ad to omit the salutation and begin with the body of the letter.

The Referral Letter

THE VALUE OF the referral letter is in its name-dropping. If you can grab the potential employer's attention by mentioning someone he knows and respects in the first line of the letter, you will have gained a terrific advantage over the competition. Some variations on the referral letter include approaches like these:

"I met with Mary Jones last week, and she mentioned that you might have need for someone with a background in book marketing."

"My adviser, Claude Brachfeld, never misses an opportunity to tell me of your innovations in the superconductivity field."

It would be a rare employer who would fail to interview an applicant with such an edge.

There is also such a thing as a self-referred cover letter, which results when you call the employer before sending a cover letter and resume. Sometimes employers will put their phone number in an ad even though they are really looking for letters and resumes, wishing to do some preliminary screening by phone. They'll ask only those who sound qualified to send their resumes. So, you call up and the employer asks you to send her your resume. When you write to her, you remind her of the conversation:

"I enjoyed chatting with you this morning about the opening in your art department. As you recall, I told you I have the experience with desktop publishing that you're looking for ..."

There are other occasions when you may find it useful to call the employer and follow up with a self-referred letter. For instance, you might call at the suggestion of a friend who works at the company and says there are openings you would be right for.

The Basics

THERE IS A formula that can be followed for cover letters. We stress can because the most important advice we can give you about this formula and the many sample cover letters at the back of this book is: Don't be afraid to deviate from the formula. Steal phrases, words, and basic structures to your heart's content, but adapt each cover letter to the specific situation. Be a professional and write your own letters.

It's critical that your letter is unique and specific to you—not one that any applicant could have written. Employers can smell a formula a mile away, yet most job-hunters insist on writing letters that sound the same as every other cover letter. As a result, most letters are insufferably dull. You'll make the employer's day if you write an interesting letter. We've had employers call us just to compliment us on our cover letters even when, for one reason or another, they weren't able to hire us.

If you're having trouble getting started, see the worksheets on pages 17 and 19.

The Cover Letter Formula

First paragraph: Tell why you're writing, in such a way as to arouse the employer's interest. Use this paragraph to display your specific knowledge about the company you're writing to.

Second paragraph: Briefly describe your professional and/or academic qualifications. Identify the job title or general area you're interested in. The reader shouldn't have to guess what kind of job you're looking for.

Third paragraph: Relate yourself to the company. Give details as to why you should be considered. Cite examples of your qualifications for the position sought. Draw on the power of your resume and refer to it—but better yet—expand on it. Avoid trite, overused phrases, such as "as you will note in my enclosed resume" or "I have taken the liberty of enclosing my resume." If you are short on job experience, mention extracurricular activities, especially examples of leadership, special projects you worked on, or the fact that you worked your way through school. If you're a homemaker returning to the workforce, don't forget to include volunteer work and family-management skills.

Fourth paragraph: Request action. Ask for an interview appointment. Suggest a time. Tell the employer that you will call to make an appointment. [Be sure to follow up!] It's a lot harder for the employer to ignore a request for

action than a wishy-washy "call me if you're interested" approach.

Before closing: Thank the prospective employer for his or her time and consideration.

Dear So and So:
To Whom Should You Send Your Letter?

The best way to find out who should receive your letter is to call the company and ask the receptionist. For example, "Could you tell me who does the hiring for financial analyst positions?" If the receptionist refers you to the personnel department, ask also for the name of the company president. If you must choose between sending your letter to a personnel director and the company president, send it to the president (unless it's a very large company, in which case you should ask for the head of the department in which you're interested in working).

Yes, it's true the president may never see that mail. A secretary or other lower-echelon staffer will probably open and screen the president's mail, but whoever handles it is responsible for responding to the president's mail and making certain the president's image isn't damaged by failing to respond to a correspondent. The underling has to report back to the president on what action was taken; thus a chain of communication is initiated centering around your letter.

Chances are your letter will end up back in the personnel office anyway, but if you send it to the president you will increase the chances of someone with real hiring power seeing it along the way.

Attention-Grabbing Beginnings:
The Twenty-Second Test

The biggest trick to composing a dynamic cover letter is to begin it in a way that will draw the reader in and make him or her want to read more—and ultimately read your resume and invite you for an interview.

Let's look at it this way: About 500 pieces of paper a week cross the desk of the average busy executive. If he or she spends 25 percent of the workday reading correspondence—and that's a very generous estimate—that means devoting one minute to each piece of paper. But many of those papers represent situations far more urgent to the executive than your cover letter, especially if it's an unsolicited one. You may have as few as twenty seconds to grab someone's attention.

Some ways to do that include beginning with a quote, starting with a clever angle (samples, pages 103–106), and praising the employer you're writing to (samples, page 89).

Quotes

Using a meaningful quote from someone in your field can be an attention-getting way to start your letter. You should be sure that the quote is truly meaningful to the job you're seeking, and was spoken by someone your reader is likely to respect. Also, make sure your quote isn't too long. No matter how good it is, if it's too long your reader is bound to wonder when you're going to get to the point, and maybe put it down halfway through.

Praising the Employer

What employer wouldn't warm up to an applicant who talks about how much she admires the company she's applying to and how much she'd like to work there—and why? Praise for the employer is often a good approach, but you can make it infinitely more credible by supporting your praise with facts that show how much you know about the firm.

The Clever Angle

Once in awhile, you may be able to come up with an approach that is out of the ordinary and shows your creativity (see samples). If you're applying for a job in a creative field such as journalism, advertising, art, or even sales, you can take more risks than if you're applying as an engineer, for instance. Again, be sure that what you're saying applies to the situation and isn't too long.

Pasting a Copy of the Ad to Your Letter

When responding to a want ad, you can direct your reader's attention to your reason for writing by pasting a copy of the want ad right on the letter. This technique is particularly effective when writing to a large company that regularly advertises openings, as the recipient can tell immediately which ad you're responding to. Seeing the ad will also refresh his or her memory about what the ad is asking for, and if you've tailored your letter well to the requirements of the ad, your reader just may end up with the impression that you're the perfect person for the job. Obviously, this is not a good approach if your qualifications don't quite match the requirements of the ad.

The Body of the Letter

Your Unique Selling Proposition

There's an advertising term that you should think about when you are composing the body of your letter: the Unique Selling Proposition, or USP. When companies are trying to determine how to market a product, they focus on the **Unique Selling Proposition,** the one thing that makes that product different from any other. It's the one reason they think consumers will buy the product even though it may seem no different from many others just like it. It may be that it has a lower price or more convenient packaging, or it may taste or smell better, or last longer.

When preparing to write a cover letter, you may find it helpful to think about your Unique Selling Proposition. What is the one thing that makes you unique? What makes you better than any other candidate applying for a similar position with this company? What can you offer that no other applicant can? What is the one reason the employer should want to hire you above all other candidates? If you can determine your Unique Selling Proposition and build it into a dynamic paragraph, you will have a real advantage in creating a dynamic cover letter.

Broadcast Your Accomplishments

To get a great deal of material for the body of your cover letters, make lists of your accomplishments in each of your past positions or in your academic career. Try to list at least three major accomplishments from each position. Think of ways that you left each company or department better than you found it. From that list, choose about three accomplishments that are most relevant to the position you're applying for.

The Screening Process

Remember that when answering ads, you should speak to the requirements of the ad. If your experience does not exactly match what is being asked for in the ad, you can sometimes still make a case for yourself in your cover letter. However, the first person who reads your letter may not have the power and wisdom to decide that you are a worthwhile candidate despite the lack of a perfect match. The first person who reads your letter may be a clerk or other subordinate, screening letters according to whether or not the qualifications

match the exact requirements stated in the ad. Therefore, it's important to make the match seem as close as possible. Pick out key phrases and adapt them to your experience.

If the person screening the letter is looking for someone with, say, two to three years of experience, it may actually hurt you if you have considerably more experience because the numbers won't match up. So, you should say you have "more than two to three years experience" so the screener will see the magic "two to three."

Turning a No into a Yes

Imagine an ad that says, "Must have experience placing press releases in publications." Let's say you don't have that particular experience, but all your other qualifications match the requirements of the ad. You might decide to write something like this: "Although I don't have experience placing press releases in publications, my experience as an editor has shown me what editors are looking for in the releases they publish." This is a step in the right direction, but a bit too negative.

To develop a more positive, sales-oriented way of addressing the lack of experience in your cover letter, picture an employer asking the same question in an interview: "Do you have experience placing press releases in publications?" If you respond, "No, but my experience as an editor, etc . . ." you automatically have a strike against you because the employer doesn't want to hear "no."

The same thing applies in your cover letter. Don't say: "Although I don't have experience placing press releases in publications . . ." Instead, simply use the rest of the sentence: "My experience as an editor has shown me what editors are looking for in the press releases they publish."

You've turned a "no" into a "yes" and made it look as though you meet the requirements of the ad when you don't quite. Yet, you were completely honest. See Stacey Greene's letter on page 23 for an example of how an applicant turns a "no" into a "yes."

The Bottom Line

The job-seeker should always remember that most businesses are there to make money. Employers would like to know that you can help them make money or at least help them not spend so much. Never lose an opportunity to tell the employer how you can make money for the company, improve sales, reduce costs, or cut waste. An easy way to remember is the PEP formula: Profitability, Efficiency, Productivity.

Two Magic Words

Two words we try not to leave out of any cover letter are "contribution" and "success." We almost always use "contribution" in the first paragraph: "My solid editing experience would enable me to make a meaningful contribution to the managing editor position you are currently advertising." This practice follows the philosophy of telling the employer what you can do for him or her, how you can help his or her bottom line. Employers like the attitude that you want to contribute to the company.

And, nothing succeeds like success. We always make a point of telling the employer how we succeeded in at least one area of our experience. "Success" is a confident word. Employers like an applicant who considers himself or herself a success.

Tips for a Dynamic Format

EMPLOYERS SCAN COVER letters quickly. Thus, anything you can do to make your special qualifications stand out will give you an edge. Three ways to accent your special qualities are highlighting, quantifying, and demonstrating your ideas.

Highlighting

Some good examples of highlighting can be found on pages 98, 99, 100, and 101 in the sample letters section. These job-seekers have used formats that make their accomplishments stand out—and make it easier for the reader to note them at a glance. Highlighting is also a great technique to use when you are tailoring your letter to the requirements of an ad (the sample letter on page 102 is a nice example of this). One way to do it is by listing special accomplishments and setting them off with bullets, which are those little marks, such as ❑, ●, and ✔. You can also set off your list by indenting it. You can highlight words, phrases, and accomplishments by underlining them or making them bold. Most typewriters can't generate bullets, but you can buy them in the form of transfer lettering (also called rub-on lettering) at most art or office-supply stores.

Quantifying

Numbers talk. Sometimes numbers are the best way to drive home a point about your achievements. Tell how many people you supervised, how many customers you handled, how much money you saved the company, by what percentage sales increased in your department during your tenure. You can also say things like:

"I was circulation director for a newspaper with a circulation of 100,000."

"My experience includes creative supervision at the largest ad agency in Tucson."

"I supervised telephone installation requests in the second-largest city in Massachusetts."

Demonstrating Your Ideas

An employer can hardly help being impressed by an applicant who has learned so much about the field and/or the company that he can offer his ideas for the company's profitability or efficiency. The best setting for an employer to hear your ideas is in the interview, but to make sure you get the interview, you might want to whet the employer's appetite by revealing a couple of ideas in your cover letter. Remember not to give away too much for free. Just tease the employer with your ingenuity enough so he'll want to hear more.

Closing Your Letter

After thanking the employer for his time and for considering you for a position, you can sign off with any of the standard business-letter closings: "Yours truly," "Very truly yours," or "Sincerely." We use "Cordially" as a friendly approach.

Don't forget to sign your letter. And do sign boldly and confidently—some experts suggest that a black or blue felt-tip pen will produce the proper bold, confident signature.

Do's and Don'ts

Don't ever send your resume without a cover letter.

Do address your letter to a named individual.

Don't use a sexist salutation, such as "Gentlemen" when answering a blind ad.

Don't be negative or too humble.

Do project confidence. For some fields, such as sales or a creative field, it may be okay for your confidence to border on cockiness. Just **Don't** be arrogant.

Don't use such cliches as "Enclosed please find my resume" or "As you can see on my resume enclosed herewith." Employers can see that your resume is enclosed; they don't need you to tell them. Such trite phrases just waste precious space.

Don't leave the ball in the employer's court. Don't say things like, "If you

are interested in someone with my qualifications, please feel free to call me to arrange an interview" or "I look forward to hearing from you." **Don't** depend on the employer to take action. Request action. Request an interview, and tell the employer when you will follow up to arrange it. Then, **Do So.** It is imperative that you follow up. You will greatly increase your chances of getting interviews if you call the employer after writing instead of sitting back and waiting for a call. Those who wait for the employer to call them will generally have a long wait indeed. When we critiqued nearly 100 cover letters that came to us online over the Internet, *not a single one* of the original letters used this proactive approach that would have greatly increased their chances of landing an interview. Thus, if you use the proactive approach, you will stand out in the crowd of cover-letter writers who meekly close by saying "I look forward to hearing from you soon."

Do make the most of your opening paragraph.

Don't send a cover letter that contains any typos, misspellings, incorrect grammar or punctuation, smudges, or grease from yesterday's lunch.

Do use simple language and uncomplicated sentence structure. Ruthlessly eliminate all unnecessary words. Follow the journalist's credo: Write tight!

Do speak to the requirements of the job, especially when responding to an ad.

Don't send letters that are obviously photocopied or otherwise mass-produced. **Do** send an original letter to each employer.

Don't include a salary requirement unless the employer requests it; even then, including any information about salary may be risky (see "Sticky Issues," page 49).

Do imagine yourself in the prospective employer's position. What would you look for in a cover letter? What would turn you off? What would you consider vital information and what would you just as soon see left out?

Do keep it brief. **Never, Never** more than one page, and it's best to keep it well under a full page. Each paragraph should have no more than four or five sentences. You may think there is important information that you can't possibly leave out, but rest assured, a busy employer will never read it all. The longer your letter appears, the more forbidding it is. If it looks hopelessly long, it may never be read at all.

Don't write your letter by hand unless the ad requests it.

Don't tell the employer what he or she can do for you. **Do** tell the employer how you can meet his or her needs and contribute to the company. This is a very common mistake among inexperienced job-hunters. (The employers may like to have happy, motivated employees, but they don't really care whether you see his company fulfilling your dreams.) Generally speaking, an employer is in business to make a profit, and wants to know how you can help do that.

To paraphrase John F. Kennedy, ask not what the company can do for you, tell what you can do for the company.

If you're a recent graduate, **Don't** forget that the employer's frame of reference is different from a professor's or admissions officer's. He or she may think it's nice that your grade-point average is high or that you got an A in a particularly tough course, but it doesn't often mean a great deal in a professional context. An employer will be more impressed that you worked your way through school and/or took advantage of every internship opportunity.

Don't be oversolicitous or plead for favors. Your qualifications should stand on their own.

Do try to answer the question that the employer is going to be asking while reading your letter: "Why should I hire this person?" Answer with your Unique Selling Proposition.

Don't rehash your resume. You can use your cover letter to highlight the aspects of your resume that are relevant to the position, but you're wasting precious space—and the potential employer's time—if you simply repeat your resume.

Don't try to include too much detail or be too general. Hone in on the pithy, precise descriptions of the accomplishments that qualify you for the job.

Don't make the employer dig through the letter to discover what kind of job you're seeking.

Don't use vague and nebulous phrases that describe your personal objectives: "I am seeking a responsible, people-oriented position with growth potential." Such a description could apply to hundreds of jobs. It's your responsibility to discover which jobs fulfill those requirements.

Don't expect the employer to offer career counseling. Once in a while, you might run into a benevolent sort who will give you some career advice in an interview. But don't ask for it in a cover letter: "I'd like the opportunity to interview with you so I can clarify my career goals."

Don't list hobbies or personal interests in your letter unless they are somehow relevant to the position, or you happen to know the person you're writing to is passionate about the same interests. We once knew someone who went through a long series of interviews for a marketing position at a golfing magazine. Just when he was sure he had the job, the magazine rejected him. The reason: He didn't play golf. Nothing he could have said in his cover letter would have gotten him the job, but if he had been a golfer and said so in his cover letter, he would have had a clear advantage.

Do be sure the potential employer can reach you. Whenever you know the name of the employer you're writing to, you should follow up and make an interview appointment. However, you should always make sure the employer

knows how to reach you in case he wants to call you for an interview before you've had a chance to follow up. If you're writing in response to a blind-box ad, you should, of course, be sure the boxholder knows how to reach you. Your letter should include a phone number that the employer can use to reach you during daytime business hours. It can be your work number if you are able to discreetly receive phone calls at your place of employment. It can be your home number if someone is there during the day to answer the phone or if you have an answering machine. Just be sure that whatever number you use is not one that will result in an unanswered phone every time the employer tries to call during business hours.

Do use action verbs. See list below.

Action verbs

accelerated	distributed	orchestrated	simplified
accomplished	doubled	organized	sold
achieved	eliminated	performed	solved
administered	enlarged	planned	sorted
analyzed	established	prepared	specialized
approved	examined	presented	stabilized
arranged	expanded	processed	started
bought	facilitated	programmed	streamlined
built	governed	promoted	strengthened
cataloged	grouped	proposed	structured
classified	guided	purchased	succeeded
completed	hired	recommended	summarized
conceived	implemented	recruited	supervised
conducted	improved	rectified	systematized
consolidated	increased	redesigned	trained
contracted	indexed	reduced	transacted
controlled	interviewed	regulated	translated
coordinated	introduced	reorganized	trimmed
created	invented	represented	tripled
decreased	investigated	researched	turned around
delivered	launched	reshaped	uncovered
demonstrated	maintained	restructured	unified
designed	managed	revised	unraveled
developed	moderated	saved	widened
devised	monitored	scheduled	won
directed	negotiated	serviced	wrote

A Cover-Letter Worksheet

T HE HARDEST PART of writing a cover letter is getting started. If you're having trouble, a worksheet like the one below may get you going. The example below shows how one job-seeker filled out the worksheet. The following page shows the letter that resulted from this worksheet. On page 19 is a blank, which you may want to photocopy and use to get started on your own letters.

Remember that the worksheet merely provides the skeleton. Once you have the bare bones, you need to develop the letter.

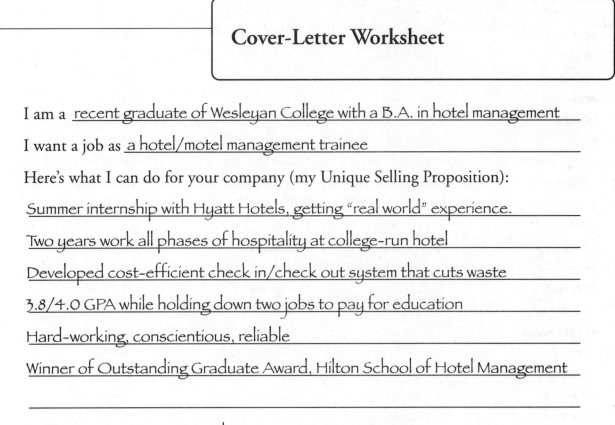

Cover-Letter Worksheet

I am a <u>recent graduate of Wesleyan College with a B.A. in hotel management</u>

I want a job as <u>a hotel/motel management trainee</u>

Here's what I can do for your company (my Unique Selling Proposition):

<u>Summer internship with Hyatt Hotels, getting "real world" experience.</u>

<u>Two years work all phases of hospitality at college-run hotel</u>

<u>Developed cost-efficient check in/check out system that cuts waste</u>

<u>3.8/4.0 GPA while holding down two jobs to pay for education</u>

<u>Hard-working, conscientious, reliable</u>

<u>Winner of Outstanding Graduate Award, Hilton School of Hotel Management</u>

I will contact you <u>next week</u> to set up an interview.

Thank you for your time and consideration.

John Donovan
435 Shoreline Drive
Charleston, SC 29407
803-555-0303

Mr. Roger G. Harlon
National Hotels
2371 Peachtree Lane, NE
Atlanta, GA 30306

Dear Mr. Harlon,

I'd like to contribute my sharp hotel-management skills, gained through years of experience and my B.A. in hospitality management, as a management trainee with your hotel chain.

I'm a recent graduate of Wesleyan College—with a grade-point average of 3.8 out of 4.0—and several years of relevant experience, including:

• Two years in varying levels learning all phases of hospitality management at a college-managed hotel.

• Summer internship with Hyatt Hotels.

I have put this experience to good use, first in developing a cost-efficient check in/check out system that cut down on waste, saving the college-run hotel an average of $5 per guest.

Second, because of this proven innovation and leadership, I won the Outstanding Graduate Award.

I am hard-working, conscientious, and reliable, and I want to put my knowledge and experience to work for your hotel chain.

I will contact you next week to set up an interview.

Thank you for your time and consideration.

Sincerely,

John Donovan

Editing

AFTER YOU'VE COMPOSED your cover letter, you should take a red pencil to it and edit mercilessly. Eliminate every unnecessary word. The more concise you can make your letter, the clearer your message will be: short, sweet, and to the point. The more you can say in the least number of words, the more likely the employer is to read and pay attention to your letter.

On the next two pages are a too-long cover letter and its edited, concise version. The job-seeker who wrote it tried to crowd his letter with too much unnecessary detail.

Mr. Salvador was justifiably proud of his academic career. As he indicates in his last paragraph, he believes his background could be useful at a newspaper. But his letter has done nothing to convince the prospective employer that there is any connection between his academic achievements and what he could do for a newspaper. He may well have a vision of how his academic background

would relate to being a municipal reporter or sportswriter, but he has done nothing in his letter to relate his college background to the job. Instead, he has told his entire academic history, although little of it has any relevance to the job he is seeking.

His other problem is that his sentences are too long and wordy. The original letter was so long that it went to two pages, a definite no-no in cover letters. Note that, even squeezed onto one page, it is far too wordy and beside-the-point. He needed to remember that his frame of reference, the academic world, is probably very different from the employer's. What sounds impressive in academia may elicit no more than a yawn from any employer seeking an experienced candidate.

While we've edited Mr. Salvador's letter primarily for length and complexity, we provide on the pages following Salvador's letter three Cover Letter Makeovers that target additional problems common to cover letters: presenting yourself as qualified for a job for which you might not seem quite qualified, writing a cover letter that helps you switch careers, and avoiding writing your autobiography in your cover letter.

A must-have source on concise writing and correct word usage is the classic Elements of Style by William Strunk and E. B. White. Macmillan puts out an inexpensive paperback edition. Get it.

To demonstrate some of the more common writing-style problems in cover letters, we've concluded this editing section with a writing-style checklist and editing exercises to help you practice your editing skills.

After you've cut your letter down to size and proofed it carefully for typos, spelling, grammar, syntax, punctuation, and capitalization, put it down for a few hours (if your time frame allows). Come back later and read it as though you were the employer. Does it grab you? Is it compelling? Would it make you want to call the applicant in for an interview?

You can also ask a friend to read your cover letter, ideally someone who has experience screening and hiring, or someone in your field.

Well-known ad executive Jane Trahey had a unique method for discovering her letters' impact. She would write her letter, stick it in an envelope, and mail it to herself. By the time it arrived, she would have virtually forgotten sending it and could approach it with the same degree of subjectivity as a prospective employer.

Sometimes merely editing for wordiness is not enough. Occasionally a cover letter requires a complete overhaul. The three letters that follow each represent a specific problem that the job-seekers try to address in their cover letters—with marginal success. We critiqued the letters and then rewrote them in a way that better targets the situations in which these job seekers find themselves.

A Letter in Need of Editing

Mrs. Karen Harper
Editor, Wonderful Publications
P.O. Box 185
Secaucus, NJ 07001

Dear Mrs. Harper,

I am interested in applying for the entry-level Municipal Reporting and Sportswriter positions advertised in the September 18, 1994 edition of the *Nutville Post*. In October of 1993, I graduated from Drew University in Madison, New Jersey with a Master of Arts degree in political science. In May of 1992, I graduated from Rutgers University with dual Bachelor of Arts degrees in political science and history. Since my October graduation, I have furthered my studies by completing several courses at Montclair State College.

Enclosed is my resume, which will give you an idea of my interests and achievements in the public affairs and communications areas. Please note that while attending Drew University, I was selected to participate in the Semester on the United Nations program. Twice weekly, I studied at the United Nations and the Drew facilities on United Nations Plaza in a program that included briefings and addresses by members of the Secretariat, the delegations, the specialized agencies, and the nongovernmental organizations represented at the United Nations. Furthermore, please note that while attending Rutgers University, I was selected to join the Iota-Alpha Chapter of Phi Alpha Theta, the International Council of Conspicuous Attainments and Scholarship in the Field of History.

In addition, please note that in selecting my curricula, I emphasized creative writing and development of oral communications skills. As a result, I am able to structure a problem into question form, provide a thesis answer, and support my thesis through qualitative and quantitative methods. Moreover, my three years on the Rutgers University Student Governing Association, two years as president and treasurer of the Rutgers University Political Science Club, and graduate training on team projects at Drew University have given me the ability to address large groups with enthusiasm and clarity.

Similarly, please note that while attending St. Bonaventure High School in Newark, I was selected to serve a three-year term as boys' basketball scorekeeper/statistician and sports-information director. As a consequence, a portion of my responsibilities included the preparation and dissemination of sports information to *The Newark Star-Ledger* and the *Jersey Journal*.

Without hesitation, please contact the following three gentlemen for references: Dr. Walter Miller 201-555-3000. Dr. Kenneth Copwell 201-555-5105. Dr. David Wicker 201-555-6485.

Since I believe my background could be utilized very effectively by your newspaper, I hope to hear from you regarding a personal interview.

Cordially,

Peter Salvador

Mrs. Karen Harper
Editor, Wonderful Publications
P.O. Box 185
Secaucus, NJ 07001

Dear Mrs. Harper,

My strong academic background in political science and government would enable me to make a significant contribution to the municipal reporting position you are currently advertising.

Municipal reporting requires the ability to translate complex governmental issues into simple language for the layperson. My academic career has made me well-versed in government issues. My ability to study and communicate about public affairs was recognized when I was chosen to participate in a special United Nations study program, and selected for membership in a history honor society.

My courses also emphasized creative writing and development of oral communications skills, which would enable me to ask politicians the right questions and communicate the issues clearly to readers.

My leadership abilities and skill in working as a team-player may be of eventual interest to you as you are promoting reporters to editing positions. I have been involved in student government, held office in a political-science club, and worked on team projects during my graduate training.

I am also interested in the sports writing position you advertised, and my three years as a school team statistician and sports-information director show I am equally capable of communicating about sports. I demonstrated my ability to assemble sports material for publication by preparing team reports for the *Newark Star-Ledger* and the *Jersey Journal*.

I'll give you a call next week to arrange a personal interview.

Cordially,

Peter Salvador

Stacey Greene
Rural Route Four, Box 645
Sparland, Illinois 61565
(309) 555-3683 (home)
(309) 555-8541 (work)

Mr. Edward Rivera
AMOCO
Chicago, IL

Dear Mr. Rivera:

I would like to apply for the marketing–research manager position that you advertised in the Chicago Tribune. I believe I could be an asset to your firm as I am very interested in such a research management position. My current position is market research and sales support. I would like to stay on the research side and move more towards management.

I feel that I am qualified and could grow into the position although I have not been employed as a research manager. However I can bring a more diverse background and a strong desire to learn. Outside of my current job I have been involved in various aspects of research projects. I have conducted survey research for a professional organization based in Chicago by utilizing the Internet as a population base. I have conducted various consulting projects for nonprofit organizations in my community. Finally, I have been involved in numerous focus groups, both as a participant and as a moderator.

While I have no direct management experience, I do believe that my background of working with people, both individually and in committees, provides me with the insight needed to be a successful manager.

Please consider me for this position as I think I could contribute a great deal. Feel free to contact me so we can get together and discuss this further.

Sincerely,

Stacey Greene
Research Analyst
Spiegel, Inc.

The Problem: Stacey Greene is answering an ad for a job for which she doesn't feel quite qualified. Her challenge is to be honest about her qualifications yet not sound too negative about her weaknesses. In other words, she wishes to turn a "no" into a "yes." What she must remember above all is that the mission of the cover letter is to help secure an interview. She doesn't have to reveal at this point every aspect of her career; she can save that for the interview. Yet, she also doesn't want to misrepresent herself.

Body of Greene's Letter, Critiqued (paragraph by paragraph)

I would like to apply for the marketing–research manager position that you advertised in the Chicago Tribune. I believe I could be an asset to your firm as I am very interested in such a research management position. My current position is market research and sales support. I would like to stay on the research side and move more towards management.

Not a bad opening, but could be tightened and restructured for greater impact.

I feel that I am qualified and could grow into the position although I have not been employed as a research manager. However I can bring a more diverse background and a strong desire to learn.

It's always a tricky situation when you're applying for a job that is a bit of a stretch. You want to be honest, but you don't want to sound too negative. Here, Greene does sound a bit too negative. She can make this sound more positive without being dishonest.

She should definitely skip the phrase "a strong desire to learn." Most companies are far more concerned with profitability, efficiency, and productivity than with teaching their employees. They don't want to be reminded of the time and money investment they have to make in new employees. Given a choice between a candidate who was fully qualified and one with "a strong desire to learn," which one do you think the employer will choose? Greene needs to make herself sound fully qualified without being dishonest. Tricky, indeed.

Outside of my current job I have been involved in various aspects of research projects. I have conducted survey research for a professional organization based in Chicago by utilizing the Internet as a population base. I have conducted various consulting projects for nonprofit organizations in my community. Finally, I have been involved in numerous focus groups, both as a participant and as a moderator.

Green can use some of this material to make the case that she is indeed qualified by moving it up higher in the letter. She should emphasize these qualifications rather than the fact that she hasn't worked as a market-research manager.

While I have no direct management experience, I do believe that my background of working with people, both individually and in committees, provides me with the insight needed to be a successful manager.

This paragraph provides the perfect opportunity to apply the "Turning a No into a Yes" technique described on page 11. By simply omitting the negative opening clause and making the rest of the sentence sound more confident, she

Stacey Greene
Rural Route Four, Box 645
Sparland, Illinois 61565
(309) 555-3683 (home)
(309) 555-8541 (work)

Mr. Edward Rivera
AMOCO
Chicago, IL

Dear Mr. Rivera:

My experience in marketing research and sales support coincides remarkably well with the details of the market research–manager position that you advertised in the Chicago Tribune.

I have conducted survey research for a professional organization based in Chicago by utilizing the Internet as a population base. I have conducted various consulting projects for nonprofit organizations in my community. Finally, I have been involved in numerous focus groups, both as a participant and as a moderator.

My background of working with people, both individually and in committees, provides me the insight needed to be a successful manager.

Please consider me for this position as I stand ready to make a considerable contribution. I will contact you in ten days to set up an appointment to meet and further discuss how my background would fit your needs.

Thank you for your consideration.

Sincerely,

Stacey Greene

makes herself a much more viable candidate for the job without being dishonest about the shortcomings in her background.

Please consider me for this position as I think I could contribute a great deal. Feel free to contact me so we can get together and discuss this further.

Greene needs to take a more proactive approach. She should not leave the ball in the employer's court. The phrase "Feel free to contact me" sounds wimpy. Greene needs to make a much stronger statement about the desirability of a meeting.

Joe Morrison
Western Massachusetts Agricultural Research
63 North Street
Deerfield, MA 02052

09.30.94

Dear Mr. Morrison:

I am applying for the Germination Research Project Manager position that was advertised in the August issue of Plant Physiologists Monthly.

Briefly, I currently hold a Postdoctoral Research Associate position at the University of Nebraska Department of Biochemistry. My research involves the purification and characterization of a protein phosphatase from the chloroplast thylakoid membrane. This enzyme is involved in dephosphorylation of the light-harvesting complex II which may regulate the State 2 to State 1 transition in photosynthetic energy distribution.

I am very interested in the announced position and feel that I possess the qualifications listed. At the University of Kentucky and at the University of Oregon I have been responsible for the general operation of the labs that I have worked in. This work has included operating and maintaining modern biochemical laboratory equipment, training others in the use of instrumentation, analyzing and reporting research results, managing part-time student workers, complying with chemical and radioisotope safety regulations, and maintaining laboratory inventory. I have excellent communication skills and work well with people from diverse backgrounds.

Although I have not had direct experience with corn, I have had extensive experience in seed physiology. Mainly, I have been responsible for research on carbohydrate and lipid metabolism and their relationship to seed germination. This research has included the separation of soluble sugars and triglycerols and the examination of in vitro translation products from isolated poly(A)+RNA. I have also had direct laboratory experience in protein purification and immunological detection of proteins. My M.S. degree research at Duke University was part of a joint research project with MacroAgro Corporation and involved assessment of pine seedling quality using various physiological indices. In college, I took 29 credits of graduate biochemistry and plant physiology courses, I have taken 10 credits of graduate statistics courses, and have been directly responsible for field and laboratory experimental design and analysis.

You will find more information about my education and research experience in the enclosed resume. Please contact me at (402) 555-2392 during business hours, or e-mail me at hmarker@unlinfo.unl.edu if you have any further questions. Thank you for considering me for the Germination Research Project Manager position.

Sincerely,

Harry Marker

The Problem: Many scientists, like Harry Marker, whose letter appears below, feel the need to provide a narrative of their entire career and all their scientific research. Like Stacey Greene, they need to realize that a cover letter should entice the employer into inviting the applicant to an interview and not become an autobiography of a life's work. Scientists, like others jobseekers, should relate their past experience to what they think they would be doing in the prospective job. Most scientists also enclose a detailed resume (called a curriculum vitae) that provides all the same information about their scientific endeavors, so it's superfluous to repeat that information in the cover letter. Harry's two-page letter is also typical of many other scientists' cover letters that we critiqued, in that the paragraphs are much too long to be easily readable.

Body of Marker's Letter, Critiqued (paragraph by paragraph)

I am applying for the Germination Research Project Manager position that was advertised in the August issue of Plant Physiologists Monthly.

This is a fairly standard, formulaic opening for a cover letter. While there is nothing wrong with such an opener per se, it will not command the attention of one written in a more interesting, attention-getting manner.

Briefly, I currently hold a Postdoctoral Research Associate position at the University of Nebraska Department of Biochemistry. My research involves the purification and characterization of a protein phosphatase from the chloroplast thylakoid membrane. This enzyme is involved in dephosphorylation of the light-harvesting complex II which may regulate the State 2 to State 1 transition in photosynthetic energy distribution.

It's obviously silly to say "briefly" when there's nothing brief about Harry's letter. He can summarize this information more concisely and save the details for his vita. If he feels his vita simply doesn't adequately describe his research, he might consider a supplemental sheet summarizing his research activities.

I am very interested in the announced position and feel that I possess the qualifications listed.

Harry should *show* the employer how he is qualified; he shouldn't just tell him.

At the University of Kentucky and at the University of Oregon I have been responsible for the general operation of the labs that I have worked in. This work has included operating and maintaining modern biochemical laboratory equipment, training others in the use of instrumentation, analyzing and reporting research results, managing part-time student workers, complying with chemical and radioisotope safety regulations, and maintaining laboratory inventory. At the University of Kentucky and at the University of Oregon I have been responsible for the general operation of the labs that I have worked in.

✉ Harry could break up this long paragraph and make it much more readable by using the highlighting techniques described on page 12.

I have excellent communication skills and work well with people from diverse backgrounds.

✉ A value judgment such as this will carry much more credibility if he can attribute it to former employers and/or professors.

Although I have not had direct experience with corn, I have had extensive experience in seed physiology.

✉ Like Stacey Greene, Harry can turn a "no" into a "yes" by omitting this negative first clause. In fact, without that clause, the sentence would be a good basis for a more attention-grabbing opening paragraph.

Mainly, I have been responsible for research on carbohydrate and lipid metabolism and their relationship to seed germination. This research has included the separation of soluble sugars and triglycerols and the examination of in vitro translation products from isolated poly(A)+RNA. I have also had direct laboratory experience in protein purification and immunological detection of proteins. My M.S. degree research at Duke University was part of a joint research project with MacroAgro Corporation and involved assessment of pine seedling quality using various physiological indices. In college, I took 29 credits of graduate biochemistry and plant physiology courses, I have taken 10 credits of graduate statistics courses, and have been directly responsible for field and laboratory experimental design and analysis.

✉ Most of this information should be in Harry's vita or research-narrative summary supplement. He should skip the breakdown of college credits, which doesn't belong in a cover letter.

You will find more information about my education and research experience in the enclosed resume. Please contact me at (402) 555-2392 during business hours, or e-mail me at hmarker@unlinfo.unl.edu if you have any further questions. Thank you for considering me for the Germination Research Project Manager position.

✉ Harry's stance is not proactive. He does not ask for an interview, but instead leaves the next move up to the employer.

Joe Morrison
Western Massachusetts Agricultural Research
63 North Street
Deerfield, MA 02052

09.30.94

Dear Mr. Morrison:

My extensive experience in seed physiology would enable me to make a valuable contribution in the Germination Research Project Manager position that was advertised in the August issue of Plant Physiologists Monthly.

My responsibilities for the general operation of the labs at the University of Kentucky and at the University of Oregon align well with what you require in a research project manager:

- operating and maintaining modern biochemical laboratory equipment;
- training others in the use of instrumentation;
- analyzing and reporting research results;
- managing part-time student workers
- complying with chemical and radioisotope safety regulations;
- maintaining laboratory inventory.

My previous employers can verify that I have excellent communication skills and work well with people from diverse backgrounds.

I currently hold a Postdoctoral Research Associate position at the University of Nebraska Department of Biochemistry, where my research involves the purification and characterization of a protein phosphatase from the chloroplast thylakoid membrane.

Described in detail in the enclosed vita is my research involving carbohydrate and lipid metabolism and their relationship to seed germination, as well as my direct laboratory experience in protein purification and immunological detection of proteins. While pursuing my M.S. degree at Duke University, I worked on a joint research project with MacroAgro Corporation, which involved assessment of pine seedling quality using various physiological indices.

I'm convinced it would be worthwhile for us to meet. I will call you in two weeks to schedule an interview. If you have any questions, please contact me at (402) 555-2392 during business hours, or e-mail me at hmarker@unlinfo.unl.edu.

Thank you for considering me for the Germination Research Project Manager position.

Sincerely,

Harry Marker

Dear Dr. Cherry,

I am seeking a new position. It can be a postdoc position, or a permanent job, or something I probably do not know about. But let me introduce myself.

My name is Andrew Taylor. I am a postdoc in the lab of Dr. Michael Cohen, Technical University, Haifa, Israel. I've been working in yeast molecular genetics for many years studying, in succession, mitotic recombination, chromosome maintenance, and cell cycle. Please find details of my scientific career in my curriculum vitae which is included in the end.

My fellowship ends next April and therefore I am looking for a new position. The trick is that I am trying to change my career to a more computerized field. I am sure that Yeast Genome project is the best place for me. And I believe the project would profit from hiring me. After so many years in yeast genetics, and with my deep interest in genome organization, I know and understand virtually every bit of the related information.

My main problem is that I do not have any formal education in computer sciences, and therefore cannot prove my knowledge by presenting papers. Nevertheless, here is a more or less complete list of my computer skills.

IBM/MS-DOS	Very deep technical level. Memory management, physical and logical data organization, program interaction, batch jobs. Several times I happened to beat our computer center in retrieving "lost" data. Of course, a lot of software including Windows with applications. I can start working with a new program in no time. I simply know, or rather feel how a program should work, and usually it is correct.
UNIX	I would say I have a good working knowledge of UNIX. I can organize my environment, I know many standard UNIX programs, can, and do write simple scripts to cover my needs and for practice.
Mac	I worked a couple of times on Mac computers, and did not find it difficult. I was able to manage from the first moment, apparently because of my good knowledge of MS-Windows.
Network	This includes working knowledge of ftp, telnet, gopher, WWW, WAIS, usenet. I am well familiar with Lynx, WinMosaic, DosLynx. I know HTML, and can organize and run a WWW site. Although I need to learn forms better.
Genetic databases	PcGene, MicroGenie, Blast, some knowledge of GCG, XHusar, and IGD. (BTW, it would be very nice to see IGD applied to yeast).

Unfortunately, I do not know programming languages. This is what I badly need, and am longing for. I would be more than happy to take courses in programming, computer architecture, and the like. I love learning, and I am quick at it.

What else? I like, and I do help people when they have computer related problems. Colleagues from all our departments come to me even though my Hebrew is pretty bad, as well as their English. I am a hard worker. Usually, I spend 12+ hours a day in the lab.

To conclude, I would consider any reasonable position in the project as long as it allows my professional growth.

Thank you for your time and consideration. And sorry for the enormous length of my letter.

The best of luck,

Andrew Taylor

The Problem: Andrew Taylor is trying to make a slight shift in his scientific career to a position that is more computer-based than his previous work. While he has had considerable experience with various kinds of computers, he has neither formal training in their use nor proof of his expertise in the form of academic publications. He includes a lengthy list of his computer skills that has no place in a cover letter. In addition, Taylor commits a number of other egregious cover-letter sins. While his letter adopts a friendly and accessible tone, it rambles and is too informal in spots. He also accentuates the negative and tells what the employer can do for him instead of what he can do for the employer.

Body of Taylor's Letter, Critiqued (paragraph by paragraph)

I am seeking a new position. It can be a postdoc position, or a permanent job, or something I probably do not know about. But let me introduce myself.

Taylor's opening is confusing and a little too informal. It also sounds as though he is willing to do anything. Employers prefer applicants to say exactly what they want to do and why they are qualified.

My name is Andrew Taylor. I am a postdoc in the lab of Dr. Michael Cohen, Technical University, Haifa, Israel. I've been working in yeast molecular genetics for many years studying, in succession, mitotic recombination, chromosome maintenance, and cell cycle. Please find details of my scientific career in my curriculum vitae which is included in the end.

Taylor needs to condense the above paragraph and the one below to get at the highlights of his career and show how it could relate to a position with this prospective employer.

My fellowship ends next April and therefore I am looking for a new position. The trick is that I am trying to change my career to a more computerized field. I am sure that Yeast Genome project is the best place for me. And I believe the project would profit from hiring me. After so many years in yeast genetics, and with my deep interest in genome organization, I know and understand virtually every bit of the related information.

> Hidden within this paragraph is some good attention-grabbing information that belongs in Taylor's earlier paragraphs.

My main problem is that I do not have any formal education in computer sciences,

> Employers don't want to hear about what problems you will bring to the job; they want to hear how you will solve their problems. They don't want to hire people who will cost them a lot of time and money to train. Taylor doesn't need to present an entire litany of his shortcomings in his cover letter, the main function of which is to get him an interview. He can be positive and yet still be honest.

and therefore cannot prove my knowledge by presenting papers. Nevertheless, here is a more or less complete list of my computer skills.

> The listing doesn't belong in Taylor's cover letter (and is omitted in this critique) and it may not even have a place in his job-seeking package at all. If he is determined to use such a list, he can instead include it as a supplement to his resume.

Unfortunately, I do not know programming languages. This is what I badly need, and am longing for.

> Here, Taylor tells the employer his own needs instead of describing how he can meet the employer's needs. The employer is mostly interested in improved profitability, efficiency, and/or productivity; Taylor's letter should describe how he could contribute in these areas.

I would be more than happy to take courses in programming, computer architecture, and the like. I love learning, and I am quick at it.

> No matter how much Taylor loves to learn or how quick he is, it will still be a burden for the employer to train him or to wait for him to be trained.

What else? I like, and I do help people when they have computer related problems. Colleagues from all our department come to me even though my Hebrew is pretty bad, as well as their English. I am a hard worker. Usually, I spend 12+ hours a day in the lab.

> This paragraph is unfocused and too informal, especially the phrase "What else?" The information about the language barriers in the lab is superfluous.

Taylor should be wary that many employers would view the more than twelve hours a day in the lab as a negative rather than a positive; they would probably prefer someone who is more well-rounded and has a life outside the lab.

To conclude, I would consider any reasonable position in the project as long as it allows my professional growth.

Again, Taylor needs to be more focused and not sound as though he is willing to do anything. Even more importantly, he must not talk about *his* professional growth but how he will contribute to the employer's growth.

Thank you for your time and consideration. And sorry for the enormous length of my letter.

Instead of apologizing, Taylor should edit his letter. A good start would be to take out the computer-skills list and make it a supplement to his vita.

Taylor also leaves the ball in the employer's court and fails to ask for an interview.

The Rewritten Version

Dear Dr. Cherry:

I am prepared to bring my years of research in yeast genetics and extensive knowledge of genome organization to your lab. I particularly would like to enhance your operations through my broad computer background when my current fellowship ends in April.

I am currently doing postdoctoral work in the lab of Dr. Michael Cohen, Technical University, Haifa, Israel. I've worked in yeast molecular genetics for many years studying, in succession, mitotic recombination, chromosome maintenance, and cell cycle.

My computer knowledge comes from extensive hands-on experience in IBM/MS-DOS, UNIX, Macintosh, networks, and genetic databases. Colleagues seek me out for my computer expertise. I have detailed my specific experience in each platform on an enclosed supplemental sheet. I am also more than willing to enhance my knowledge by taking courses in such areas a programming and computer architecture.

I believe it would be mutually beneficial for us to meet. I will contact you in ten days to arrange a meeting. Should you have any questions before that time, you may reach me during business hours at the phone number shown on my vitae.

Thank you for your time and consideration.

Best regards,

Andrew Taylor

Writing-style guidelines for editing your cover letter:

Bᴇᴄᴀᴜsᴇ ᴇᴅɪᴛɪɴɢ ɪs an acquired skill, we've included a number of exercises that you can use to sharpen your writing-style editing skills before you tackle one of your own letters. Apply the checklist that follows to the exercises. Then we'll show you how we edited and rewrote the same passages.

Some style tips for cover letters include:

✔ Use active voice over passive voice. The active voice leads to lively, concrete writing, while the passive voice leads to abstraction. Learn to convert weak passive sentences into strong active ones.

Weak Passive: My experience was greatly increased due to two summer internships I had.

Strong Active: The two summer internships I completed add to my experience.

✔ As suggested on page 16, use action verbs to provide a more vivid and dynamic picture of your accomplishments.

Nonaction: I did a number of projects for the engineering department.

Action: I performed a number of successful projects for the engineering department ... OR

I completed a number of successful projects ... OR

I developed a number of successful projects ...

✔ Keep sentences short and concise. Brief, simple sentences keep the reader's attention. Long, wordy, and overly complex sentences tend to distract the reader.

Long Sentence: While completing my internship, I had the opportunity to be involved in a number of different activities, ranging from revamping the main management information system to long-range computer-needs assessment, as well as handling personnel decisions and day-to-day operations of the MIS department.

Short Sentences: During my internship I assisted in the revamping of the main information system and conducted a long-range computer-needs assessment study. I also managed the MIS department.

✔ Similarly, avoid long paragraphs. A key to your cover letter's appearance is a welcoming look, not one that appears forbidding because of lengthy paragraphs. The simple solution is to keep paragraphs to a maximum of one to two sentences. Another way to break up your paragraphs for greater readability is to use a bullet format (see section on highlighting, page 12).

Long Paragraph: While serving as marketing manager for Nabisco Products, Inc., I developed a distribution model that increased sales by more than $200,000, I pioneered an inventory tracking system that saved the cracker division more than $100,000 in lost units, and supervised the development of a ground-breaking advertising campaign. Furthermore, I was responsible for managing a staff of forty people, guiding a department budget that exceeded $1 million, and producing numerous sales and marketing reports for top management. Besides this experience, I have a bachelor's degree from Stetson University and an MBA from Harvard. As you can see, the combination of my experience and education would make me an invaluable person to head your new product division, and I would like to suggest that we schedule a meeting as soon as possible to discuss the possibility.

Short Paragraph: While serving as marketing manager for Nabisco Products, Inc., I developed a distribution model that increased sales by more than $200,000; pioneered an inventory-tracking system that saved the cracker division more than $100,000 in lost units; and supervised the development of a ground-breaking advertising campaign. I was responsible for managing a staff of forty, guiding a department budget exceeding $1 million, and producing numerous sales and marketing reports for top management.

Or **Bullet Format (Highlighting):**

While serving as marketing manager for Nabisco Products, Inc., I:

- developed a distribution model that increased sales by more than $200,000;
- pioneered an inventory-tracking system that saved the cracker division more than $100,000 in lost units;

- supervised the development of a ground-breaking advertising campaign;
- managed a staff of forty;
- guided a department budget exceeding $1 million; and
- produced numerous sales and marketing reports for top management.

I have a bachelor's degree from Stetson University and an MBA from Harvard. My combined experience and education would make me an invaluable person to head your new-product division. I would like to suggest that we schedule a meeting as soon as possible to discuss the possibility.

✔ Use parallel construction. One of the tools for making longer sentences clear and readable is to use parallel construction. Place similar ideas within your sentences and use the same grammatical construction for each.

Unparallel: My skills include that I am a team player, hard-working, motivated, and a self-starter.

Parallel: I am a highly motivated, hard-working self-starter, who believes in being a team player.

✔ Avoid unnecessary words. Pleonasms, as explained on page 41, use more words than are necessary to express an idea.

Pleonastic: My job included developing reports on a monthly basis.

Tight: My job included developing monthly reports.

✔ Check for coherence. A confusing or puzzling sentence can be a disaster in a cover letter. A sentence is coherent if all components of the sentence are logically related to all other components of the sentence.

Incoherent: Involved in the hospital even while still in school, I developed several new procedures that the psychology department at Johnstown Hospital implemented.

Coherent: While still in school, I developed several new procedures that the psychology department at Johnstown Hospital implemented.

 ✔ Check spelling and punctuation. Now that most word-processing software programs are equipped with spell-checking and grammar-checking programs, computer-using job-seekers have virtually no excuse for spelling or punctuation

errors. Keep in mind, however, that you cannot rely on these checkers to find correctly spelled, but misused, word forms.

Incorrect:	I was highly involved in there accounting department's overhaul. Its quiet an experience to see how technology can improve efficiency—and moral to..
Correct:	I was highly involved in their accounting department's overhaul. It's quite an experience to see how technology can improve efficiency—and morale too.

Our editing/rewriting checklist for dynamic cover letters. Did you:

✔ Change passive to active voice?

✔ Use action verbs?

✔ Keep sentences short?

✔ Keep paragraphs short?

✔ Use parallel construction?

✔ Avoid unnecessary words?

✔ Check for coherence?

✔ Check spelling and punctuation?

Editing Exercises:

Don't forget to keep in mind not just writing style but all the other principles of a good cover letter!

1. The following is an actual letter written in response to a classified advertisement. How would you improve it?

Currently employed as administrative assistant to one of my company's vice presidents, I am seeking employment where my secretarial, administrative and management background can be better utilized.

Now you rewrite it:

_____

_____

_____

Now, here's how we would rewrite the same paragraph. Compare how you rewrote the paragraph to the way we rewrote it.

My strong secretarial, administrative, and management background would enable me to build on the experience I've acquired as administrative assistant to one of my company's vice presidents.

Here's the second paragraph from the same letter:

Having graduated from the University of Indiana in June, I believe my comprehensive relative experience and interpersonal contact I gained through extracurricular and summer job involvement has prepared me extremely well for an executive administrator career.

Now you rewrite it:

_____

_____

_____

Now, here's how we would rewrite the same paragraph. Compare how you rewrote the paragraph to the way we rewrote it.

My comprehensive experience and degree from the University of Indiana have prepared me extremely well for an executive administrator career. I also gained interpersonal skills through extracurricular activities and summer jobs.

2. The following is an actual letter that tries to use a clever angle. The job-seeker wrote it to a computer company. See how you can improve it.

In the chronology of computers, starting in the 1940s with the development of the first general purpose digital computer through the 1950s and the development of the UNIVACs through the 1960s and the development of COBOL through the 1970s and the development of fourth-generation integrated circuits through the 1980s and the development of the Macintosh computer to the 1990s and beyond and the development of super-chips and artificial intelligence, you and your companies have been significant players in the development of the computer and the "computer age."

Now you rewrite it:

_____

_____

_____

Now, here's how we would rewrite the same paragraph. Compare how you rewrote the paragraph to the way we rewrote it.

In the chronology of computers, you and your companies have been significant players in the development of computers and the "information age."

Here's the second paragraph from the same letter:

I am writing to you because my main objective as a computer programmer is to associate with a firm that is truly in the mainstream of computer technology. At present, as you will note on my enclosed resume, I am associated with Futuristic Computers, Inc., as a senior designer and programmer. This position affords me very heavy experience in all phases of hardware and software development.

Now you rewrite it:

_____

_____

_____

Now, here's how we would rewrite the same paragraph. Compare how you rewrote the paragraph to the way we rewrote it.

My objective as a computer programmer is to contribute my skills and experience to a firm that is truly in the mainstream of computer technology.

I am currently associated with Futuristic Computers, Inc., as a senior designer and programmer. Here, I've acquired considerable experience in all phases of hardware and software development.

3. The following is an actual letter written to a financial-services company by a recent college graduate. How would you improve it?

This August I will be graduating from the University of Mexico with a bachelor's degree in finance and am seeking an opportunity to use my background. I am writing to ask if you anticipate any such openings at your company in the near future.

Now you rewrite it:

_____

_____

_____

Now, here's how we would rewrite the same paragraph. Compare how you rewrote the paragraph to the way we rewrote it.

I will graduate in August from the University of New Mexico with a bachelor's degree in finance. I am writing to ask if you anticipate any openings in which I could contribute my finance background to enhance your company's success.

Here's the second paragraph from that same letter.

Based on my experience working part-time with a local house, I feel I would be an asset to your company. Becoming a member of your finance staff would fulfill my goal of becoming a professional and would give me the opportunity to grow as a business leader.

Now you rewrite it:

_____

_____

_____

Now, here's how we would rewrite the same paragraph. Compare how you rewrote the paragraph to the way we rewrote it.

My part-time experience with a local brokerage house would be an asset to your company.

4. The following is an actual letter to a computer company by a recent college graduate. See how you can improve it.

I am a recent college graduate who is looking to enter the computer field. In view of my academic record (3.89/4.0), my program emphasis on computer languages, and my specific interest in computers, I strongly believe you should consider employing me in the computer pool at Apex Computers, Inc.

Now you rewrite it:

_____

_____

_____

Now, here's how we would rewrite the same paragraph. Compare how you rewrote the paragraph to the way we rewrote it.

I am a recent college graduate intending to enter the computer field. My curricular emphasis on computer languages combined with my strong academic record qualify me well for a position in the computer pool at Apex Computers, Inc.

Here's the second paragraph from the same letter:

Of particular interest to me is the opportunity to offer my related experience in technical and research writing, as well as my extensive education knowledge of the subject. For example, my senior-year research thesis examined how personal computers could be used in the classroom, a project where my technical writing skills excelled. My thesis was then printed and distributed to all the professors at the university.

Now you rewrite it:

_____

_____

_____

Now, here's how we would rewrite the same paragraph. Compare how you rewrote the paragraph to the way we rewrote it.

Of particular interest to me is the opportunity to offer my related experience in technical and research writing. For example, my senior-year research thesis examined how personal computers could be used in the classroom. The thesis was deemed so good, that my major professor had it distributed to the entire university faculty.

Pleonasms

A PLEONASM IS THE use of more words than are necessary to express an idea. Eliminate all unnecessary words. Go through your letters and cut out all extraneous words and phrases—then, go through and do it again. See below for a list of common pleonasms and how they can be shortened.

Pleonastic	Tight
in light of the fact that	since, because
for recycling purposes	for recycling
one particular youngster	one child, a child
on a daily basis	daily
a Career Fair to be held May 15	Career Fair May 15
symposium, which will be held on October 20	symposium October 20
in the lobby itself	in the lobby
during that period of time	when
at this point in time, at the present time	now (even "now" may be unnecessary)

Pleonastic	Tight
in order to, in an effort to	to
for the purpose of	for
graphics department, which is located in the Knott Building	graphics department in Knott Building
end result	result
utilized (not so much pleonastic as jargony)	used

Mechanics

So, YOU'VE COMPOSED the perfect cover letter ... good for you! Now you need to determine how you'll type it, what kind of paper you'll type it on, what kind of envelope you'll mail it in, and even when you should mail it.

Typing Options

EACH COVER LETTER you send must be—or appear to be—a freshly typed original. If you're sending out a lot of cover letters, typing each one individually can be a problem if you are not a great typist. It becomes even more of a problem when you realize each letter must be absolutely flawless. What are your alternatives if you don't type well?

• You can hire a typing service or resume company to type them for you. Doing so, however, can be expensive if you are mounting a mass mailing to cold contacts or if your job search takes a while and you are regularly answering many ads.

• You can rent a high-quality electric or electronic typewriter or word-processor. Many copy shops and libraries, especially in college towns, have in-house typewriters that you can rent by the hour for use on the premises. Make sure the equipment can make corrections that will be undetectable to your recipients.

• You can buy, rent, or borrow a computer whose software handles word-processing functions (or hire someone who has one). Many computer stores will allow you to lease on a fairly short-term basis. Most personal computers are relatively easy to learn to use, even for someone without a "high-tech" orientation, and chances are the store will offer training. Computerized word processing allows you to type your entire letter and then make all corrections and perfect the layout before you print it out. A computer is your best bet—if you can afford it—especially for mass mailings. You can write virtually the same letter to any number of employers, inserting individual names, addresses, and perhaps interchangeable paragraphs that demonstrate your knowledge of each company.

If You Must Use a Typewriter . . .

Beg, borrow, or buy the best one you can. An electronic typewriter with a film ribbon and a correcting feature is best. If the best you can do is a clunky old manual with a fabric ribbon, at least clean the keys and buy a fresh new ribbon. If you make a mistake, you might be able to get away with one tiny fix with correcting fluid (such as Liquid Paper or Wite-Out) or correction paper (such as Ko-Rec-Type)—but you're better off retyping the letter. There is one trick you can try, however, if you're a lousy typist. Go ahead and make your corrections with correcting fluid, but before signing, have your corrected letter copied onto nice paper at a copy shop using a high-quality machine. The copy will look like an original and the corrections will no longer be visible.

If You Use a Computer
(or hire someone to do so) . . .

Consider using the best printer you can afford. If possible, the best option is to have your letter laser-printed. If you don't have access to a laser printer (whether at home, school, or work), you can always put your letter on a computer disk and have a high-quality printout made at a copy shop or computer store for about a dollar a page. Keep in mind that appearance is extremely important, and it is better to spend a few dollars up front than to turn an employer off with a letter that is difficult to read because it is poorly printed. For state-of-the-art quality, laser printing produces a sharp, clear image. A laser printer offers many options in type, graphics, and type of paper.

Other printing options are open to you, however. The least expensive printer produces **dot-matrix** type, made up, as the name implies, of little dots. Quality varies among dot-matrix printers, and they should primarily be used for cover-letter drafts.

The next step up in printers are those that produce **letter-quality** print (LQP), such as ink-jet printers. These printers also produce type made up of dots, but they are configured in such a way that they generally resemble laser quality. An advantage with LQP printers over dot-matrix is that you have some flexibility with type face, graphics, and type of paper.

Paper

For purity and simplicity, nothing beats the classic white 8½ x 11 bond paper, with a 25 percent rag or cotton content. You can't lose by using it. However,

many variations are acceptable: ivory, cream, buff, gray, light blue, and tan are all perfectly respectable cover-letter colors. You can also use a textured finish, such as "laid" or "linen." The standard advice is not to use any really flamboyant color, but you could probably get away with an offbeat color if you're applying for a job in a creative field. You don't even really need to use a rag-content bond. The kind of bond paper used in most office copiers should be acceptable in most cases, except for professions such as law. But here's what's not acceptable:

- **Paper of a nonstandard size.** Some job-seekers send letters on 8½ by 14 paper (legal size) or 7 x 10 (monarch size) or some other odd size in the hope of making their letter stand out. All you really succeed in doing with a nonstandard size is annoying the employer because your letter sticks out of the stack, falls out of the pile, or is hard to file.

- **Social stationery.** It should go without saying that scents, flowers, and cartoon-decorated stationery have no place in the business world.

- **Your current company letterhead.** We once read an article that actually advised job-seekers to write their cover letters on their current employer's letterhead to prove they were employed. To an employer receiving a cover letter on company letterhead, the message is: "This person steals supplies from his company. He would probably steal them from me, too."

- **Corrasable or onionskin paper.** Corrasable paper, which has a slick, shiny surface that is easy to erase, does not make a very professional appearance. And onionskin is too thin and flimsy.

Envelopes

The standard #9 or #10 envelope, either white or a color and texture matching your cover letter/resume stationery, is best. If you have many enclosures, such as writing samples, lists of references and a salary history, a 9 x 12 envelope is acceptable, and keeps the materials within flat. By the time the person with hiring power gets your letter, the envelope will most likely be long gone, so it is a fairly unimportant part of your sales package.

The Perfect Package

If you can afford it, the following makes a terrific package that may impress an employer:

- Your cover letter typed on a personalized letterhead
- Your resume on a matching letterhead of the same type of paper
- An envelope in matching paper with your name and return address printed in the left-hand corner
- An attractive commemorative stamp

Although this sort of presentation may give you the ever-so-slightest edge, the advantage compared to the expense is probably negligible. Therefore, we stress that such a package is completely unnecessary. Its real advantage is to make you feel good about the image you're presenting. High morale and self-esteem are crucial in the job search.

When to Mail

Since the best and most plentiful want ads appear in the Sunday newspaper, you are likely to be writing cover letters that day. Should you mail them right away? The answer is an unequivocal yes when you are responding to a blind-box number ad, for the simple reason that the employer has rented the box for only a limited amount of time, sometimes as little as a week. For other ads, you may be better off mailing your letter as late as Tuesday so it won't get lost in the pack of letters that other job seekers mailed Sunday to arrive Tuesday. we always found we could pay more attention to the stragglers that came after the bulk of ad responses. For cold-contact mailings, some career experts have suggested you target your letters to arrive between Tuesday and Thursday, the days the power person is most likely to be at his or her desk. Tuesday has also been cited as an attractive day because it is a lighter mail day in business. The Christmas season, between Thanksgiving and New Year's Day is likely to get the least attention, so avoid this time and any other weeks with holidays in them, if you can.

Delivery Stunts

You can sometimes make an impression by having your letter hand-delivered by messenger (if the employer is in the same city) or air-expressed to another city. Neither method is cheap, but if it's the job of your dreams and there is a special reason for you to respond quickly, you may want to spring for one of these methods. If your primary motive is to impress the employer with the trouble and expense you've gone to, be aware that it may be the secretary and not the power person who knows you used a special kind of delivery.

Some career experts have suggested you can gain an advantage by marking "Personal" or "Confidential" on the envelope and even go so far as leaving your return address off. The idea is to keep a secretary from screening your letter and to arouse the employer's curiosity. Use this technique, however, at your own risk, since many employers may be more annoyed than intrigued.

Keeping a Record

IT'S A GOOD idea to keep a record of every cover letter you send out so you know when you need to follow up with which employers. There are three easy ways to keep a record.

1. Make a photocopy of every letter you send. If you have been pasting a copy of the want ad to your letter, you'll also have a record of the ad. Another good reason to make copies of your letters is that if you're not producing them on a machine with a memory (such as an electronic typewriter or computer), keeping copies will allow you to recycle paragraphs in future letters.

2. Since it's not always convenient—or cheap—to make a copy of every letter, consider buying a pad of columnar-ruled paper (or just making some vertical rule lines on notebook paper). You can make a column each for: position, company name and address (if known), name of contact person and phone number for follow-up, date you sent your cover letter/resume, and what follow-up action you took. You can also record the history of each cover letter/resume on an index card.

Using Cover Letters Creatively

YOU CAN EXPAND your networking opportunities by writing cover letters to organizations other than direct employers and making other creative uses of your cover letters.

• **Letters to your college placement service.** Such letters are particularly practical after you've graduated and moved away from your college town. A well-written letter will impress your placement officer and possibly get you preferential treatment. Some placement offices also serve nonalumni. See sample, page 85.

• **Letters to professional and trade organizations.** Almost all professional and trade organizations have some type of placement service, whether they make your resume available to member companies, publish situation-wanted ads in the group's newsletter or run a job hotline. Sometimes there is a charge for the service, sometimes not. You can send your resume with a nice cover letter to all the organizations in your field. Don't forget general professional organizations for women and minorities, such as Business and Professional Women's Association or the National Association of Black Law Enforcement Officers. Sample, page 97.

• **Letters to employment agencies.** Employment agencies frequently advertise just as direct employers do, and it should be noted that 10 percent of job-hunters at the managerial and executive level get jobs through employment agencies and executive-search firms. You can answer their ads with a cover letter that is not substantially different from one you would send an employer. The only difference is you should acknowledge that you are applying for a position with the agency's client company. You can also write cold-contact letters to agencies, especially those specializing in your field. This is not a particularly effective way to find a job, but in an extensive job search, it is another way to ensure you have covered all the bases. You will have considerably better luck if you follow up these uninvited letters to agencies with phone calls.

• **Letters to executive-search firms.** Job-seekers generally don't seek out search firms: instead, executive-search firms rely on contacts in the business world to refer candidates who will fill the needs of their client companies. These companies usually keep search firms on retainer. However, it never hurts to send your resume to an executive-search firm, especially if you are able to use the referral-letter approach. Sample, page 96.

• **Sending a letter without a resume.** Some experts suggest you send a letter without a resume because when many employers see a resume with a letter, they assume you are unemployed and sending similar mailings to a number of people. If you can summarize relevant highlights of your experience in a letter so well-written that the employer will want to talk with you further, you may be better off not sending a resume. That way your correspondence will seem more like a business letter than the run-of-the-mill resume mailing, just like the hundreds of others that cross the employer's desk. You can ask for a meeting instead of an interview.

• **Responding to a hidden opportunity in an ad.** You might see an ad for a position you're not qualified for, but you can see a hidden opportunity in the ad. For instance, one woman saw an ad for a museum-director position that she did not qualify for, but since it was in the natural-history field, where she did have considerable experience, she wrote a letter suggesting she would make a great assistant to the new director. She got the job. The same thing worked for another woman when she saw an ad seeking people to sell advertising space for a new magazine. She wasn't interested in selling, but she knew that after some ads were sold, the magazine would need an editorial staff. She wrote offering her editorial services, and she, too, was successful in creating a position for herself.

• **Informational interviews.** Use your cover letter to ask for an informational interview. While this technique is especially effective if you are a new graduate unsure of the type of job you want or are switching careers, it can work for all job-seekers by uncovering the hidden job market. The technique

is simple. Introduce yourself in your letter and, instead of asking for a job interview, ask for a small amount of the employer's time for an informational interview. While you might have to wait awhile before a busy executive can schedule an appointment with you, most employers are happy to oblige since they know you don't plan to talk them into hiring you.

At the interview, find out as much as possible about the company, its operations, needs, plans, and challenges. Find out about the kinds of positions within the company and what plans might be afoot either for expansion or downsizing. Leave your resume if it seems appropriate, but don't be pushy. You will then be armed with all the information you need to target the company with an uninvited letter in the future. You may even be able to use that letter to propose a new position after you've identified a need within the company based on the information gathered during your interview.

Yours won't exactly be a cold-contact letter, because now you know someone important in the company. Whether the company has an opening or whether you propose a new position, the employer will be much more likely to consider hiring you because he or she has already met you. You are a known quantity. The informational interview is also a great networking tool because even if the employer doesn't have an opening, he or she may refer you to someone who does.

Richard Bolles has an excellent section on informational interviewing in his classic *What Color is Your Parachute?*, described in the "Recommended Reading" section, page 143. See also the sample letter asking for an informational interview on page 134 of this book.

• **Seeking consulting and freelance opportunities.** You can use your cover letter as the writer on page 114 has—to solicit freelance and consulting assignments. A direct-mail campaign seeking these kinds of opportunities is an excellent networking tool, and freelance assignments always have the potential to turn into full-time jobs. If nothing else, these assignments will keep food on the table while you look for a full-time position.

• **Zap your cover letter into cyberspace.** Vast new opportunities to network electronically over the Information Superhighways are opening up every day. See "New Sources of Job Leads on the Information Superhighway," page 65.

Sticky Issues

WHAT IF AN ad asks for salary requirements or history? The request for salary requirements is a common problem in the writing of cover letters, especially responses to blind-box ads. Employers often use blind-box ads as a way to screen out applicants who want a bigger salary than the company feels it can or wants to pay. At the other end of the spectrum, employers sometimes eliminate from consideration those who ask for a salary much lower than what the position pays. Instead of being viewed as a bargain, the low-priced applicant is often considered to be at a lower level than the kind of person the employer seeks. The employer asks you to put your salary requirement in your cover letter, and if you want too much money, you probably won't get called for an interview. You don't know who the employer is, so there's no reason for the company to bother sending you a polite rejection letter.

If salary is the most important issue to you, you have no problem. You can put your salary requirement in your cover letter with no qualms because if the employer eliminates you, you will have lost nothing because you don't want to work for less than your required salary anyway.

If, however, the job itself is important to you and you are flexible about salary, you have more of a problem. The perfect job could be advertised. You really want it, but the blind-box ad asks for a salary requirement. If you put down your ideal salary, you risk being eliminated from a job you'd love to have.

Your choices:

• You could skirt the issue entirely by either leaving out the salary requirement or saying: "My salary requirement is negotiable." Or: "I am earning the market value for a systems analyst with four years of experience. I would be happy to discuss my compensation requirement in an interview." Be aware that some advertisers put the disclaimer in their ads that no applicant will be considered without a salary requirement. New research shows, however, that many, if not most, employers will still consider you if you omit the salary requirement. (The studies indicate that few applicants ever hear from a company that absolutely insists on a salary requirement.) Since you are "damned if you do and damned if you don't," you might as well take the approach with which you are most comfortable.

• You could state your current salary and say it is negotiable. "I am currently earning an annual salary of $25,000, and my salary requirement is negotiable." That way, if the company is planning to pay less than your current salary,

chances are you don't want the job no matter how wonderful it is.

• You could give a range, for which the low-end figure is 10 percent above your current or last salary. An employer who asks for a salary history, is trying to determine the size and frequency of raises you are accustomed to. You run the same risks with a salary history as you do with a salary requirement. If you decide to include the history, do it on a separate sheet of paper so you won't take up space in your cover letter.

Should you include references in your cover letter?

No. References belong in the interview phase of job-hunting, so they should not be listed in your resume or cover letter. Occasionally, an ad will specify that you must send references. In that case, it is probably best to list them on a separate sheet rather than take up precious space in your cover letter. You can, of course, refer to the sheet in your letter. ("A list of references is enclosed.")

Should you send letters of recommendation?

Generally no. Letters of recommendation have little credibility because anyone who would write you a letter of recommendation wouldn't say anything negative about you.

Should you explain negative aspects of your job history?

Another tough question. In the beginning of this book, we said the cover letter is an opportunity to explain the negatives. However, we must caution you to bring up any negatives extremely judiciously. Most are better handled in the interview, and you can wait for the employer to bring them up instead of calling attention to something they might not have noticed.

Chances are, whatever "problem" you think might exist with your job history is probably in your head, or at least a lot more important to you than to the prospective employer. There is no point to making your problem into the employer's problem. When in doubt, leave it out.

Don't say anything about not having enough experience. Make the most of the experience you do have and let employers judge for themselves.

Don't mention any negative circumstances of leaving any of your past jobs. One letter we received gets off to a horrendous start by telling the employer in the first sentence that the applicant was laid off from his last job. What a turnoff.

It is probably not necessary to point out lack of educational qualifications. One letter-writer wrote the following plea for consideration despite her lack of a college degree, which was included in the ad as a requirement for the job:

"Will you consider someone with the qualities you are looking for and great experience but less than four years of college?"

We believe the writer would have been better off omitting that paragraph. She could have let her otherwise good cover letter and fine resume stand on their own merits. If the employer was impressed with her experience, he might not have even looked at her educational background. If he liked her letter and resume, he might have decided that a degree really wasn't important for doing the job.

It can't hurt to briefly explain why you are making a career switch, especially if you are making a radical shift from one field to another. The sample on page 105 shows an effective way to explain career shifts.

Follow-up Letters

Post-interview Thank-You Letters

TERRIFIC. You got an interview. Now, the minute you get home, do not pass Go, do not collect $200. Instead, sit down and write a thank-you letter to the employer while the interview is fresh in your mind. If you know the employer is planning a quick decision, you may want to make special arrangements to have your thank-you letter delivered quickly, such as hiring a messenger service or even hand-delivering the letter to the employer's secretary.

Thanking a prospective employer for his or her time is just common courtesy. But, a thank-you letter can do more:

• It's a way to keep your name in front of the employer.

• It's a way to build on the strengths of the interview and emphasize the match between you and the job, especially now that you know more about the company.

• It's a way to bring up anything you thought of after the interview that is pertinent to the employer's concerns.

• If you are extremely careful, you may be able to address anything that went badly in the interview and try to correct it.

• If the employer has asked for additional materials that you didn't bring to the interview (references, writing samples, etc.) you can send a thank-you letter with the items.

• It's a way to restate your understanding of the next step in the process. ("I look forward to meeting with your vice president, Mrs. Green, sometime next week.")

• It's an opportunity to restate your interest in and enthusiasm for the job.

• It's another chance to show how well you express yourself.

But the best thing about thank-you letters is that, even though virtually every book on job-hunting advises sending thank-you letters, very few job-seekers actually do so. If you're one of the few that do, you're bound to have an edge.

See sample thank-you letters beginning on page 135.

When you get a rejection letter without an interview or after an interview

WRITE BACK TO thank the employer for acknowledging your letter or thank him again for the interview. Encourage the company to make good on its promise to keep your resume on file. The employer will be impressed with your courtesy and continuing interest. You'll keep the dialogue going with the company, and your name will more likely be remembered the next time there's an opening.

Sample follow-up to a rejection letter

34 Easy Street
St. Joseph, MO 64503
816-555-4334

Ms. Suzanne Lee
Rehabilitation Hospital
10 Medical Court
St. Louis, MO 63188

Dear Ms. Lee,

Thank you for your letter dated April 17th. I am disappointed that because of the reorganization of the department that the medical records clerk position is no longer available.

I appreciate your offer to keep my resume on file. I am very interested in working for a leader in medical care such as Rehabilitation Hospital.

Once again, thank you for your time and consideration. Good luck in the reorganization, and I hope to hear from you in the near future.

Sincerely yours,

Deborah S. Stiles

Declining Letters

YOU GOT A job offer! But, alas, the job is not right for you. The money isn't right, or another offer is better. Write a nice letter turning down the job. You never know when you might need that employer again, so you want to stay in his or her good graces.

Sample Declining Letter

409 Third Avenue
New York, NY 10010
212-555-2121

Mr. Jerry Kudos
American Graphics
12 West 15th Street

Dear Mr. Kudos,

Thank you for all the time you and Ms. Atwood spent considering me for a position as a graphic artist. I sincerely appreciate your consideration—as well as that of your staff members who spent time with me during this process.

I most appreciate your offer of employment, however, after much deliberation and careful analysis, I must respectfully decline your offer. I feel another opportunity better matches my qualifications and career path.

This has been a very difficult decision; yours was an outstanding opportunity.

I hope our paths will cross again in the future. You have been most kind, and I again thank you for your time and consideration.

Sincerely,

Mary Beth Rider

Acceptance Letters

IT'S THE MOMENT we've all been waiting for! You got an offer, and it's the perfect job! You've decided to go for it. Congratulations! It's important to write a letter thanking the employer for the offer and accepting the offer. The most

important reason to write an acceptance letter is to state your understanding of the terms of employment: salary, benefits, starting date, perquisites, duties, and so forth. That way, if there is a discrepancy between your understanding and your new employer's, it can be brought out in the open before you start work. It's also a written document that may help if legal difficulties ever arise.

Sample Acceptance Letter

145 Kelly Lane
Rochester, NY 14620
716-555-14604

Mr. Jack G. Wallace
Eastman Kodak
Colorfast Drive

Dear Mr. Wallace,

Thank you for your telephone call of September 4 offering me a job as a chemical engineer with your processing department at an annual salary of $35,000. Please consider this letter my formal acceptance.

As I mentioned to you, because I am a group leader in a major experiment with my present company, I will not be able to start until the middle of October.

The offer fulfills one of my career goals—working for Kodak.

I want to thank you for all your help and consideration. I also appreciate the help of Dr. Adams and Ms. Graf.

Please let me know if there is any additional information needed or details I should be aware of prior to my arrival in October.

Cordially,

Darlene P. Hopps

Cover Letter Hall of Shame

WE HOPE WE'VE taught you in the preceding pages everything you need to know to write a great cover letter. If you're still unclear about how to distinguish an effective letter from one bound for the circular file, we offer some additional characteristics of an inferior cover letter, followed by two samples of what not to write—the two worst cover letters we've ever seen.

Characteristics of an Ineffective Cover Letter

Your cover letter won't get much attention if:

• Its opening paragraph is boring and formulaic:

> In response to your advertisement in the National Ad Search, September 10, '94, please consider my resume in your search for a Mechanical Engineer.

> I am seeking a full time position in which I may use my prior work experience. I would be interested in exploring the possibility of obtaining such a position with your company as a Research Scientist.

> Please find enclosed a copy of my current curriculum vitae, list of publications, statement on teaching philosophy and experience, and a summary of research interests for your consideration for a faculty position in cell biology.

Ho hum. While a typical cover-letter opening, such as those above, is not *wrong*, it is simply not as effective as one that makes the employer sit up and take notice.

• It is more than one page, or the paragraphs are too long and deadly to be readable or inviting.

• You try to write your autobiography instead of a sales letter that entices the employer to call you in for an interview.

• You dilute the power of your sales message with such phrases as "I think" or "I feel." Note how much stronger the sentence below is without "I feel."

Before:	With this broad-based background I feel that I have the necessary skills to contribute significantly to your organization's success.
After:	With this broad-based background, I have the necessary skills to contribute significantly to your organization's success.

• You ask for an entry-level job. If you're a new college graduate, chances are you may end up in an entry-level job. But why advertise what sounds like a lack of ambition?

• You make unsubstantiated value judgments about yourself. There's nothing wrong with saying:

I'm extremely well-organized and a hard worker.

Consider, however, how much more power such a statement has if you can substantiate it through professors or former employers:

Any of my previous employers can attest to the fact that I'm a well-organized hard worker.

(Be sure they really can attest to those attributes!)

• You dwell on what the employer can do for you instead of what you can do for the employer.

Before: I feel that a post at your center would enable me to widen my experience and achieve my career goals.

After: I would like to contribute my experience and assist the center in reaching its goals.

• You include an unsolicited salary request.

• You include unnecessary and negative information. One job-seeker had written three wonderfully effective paragraphs. Suddenly, his letter fell apart when he wrote:

My most recent experience was with a wood-furniture manufacturer. The firm was experiencing financial difficulties when I joined them. Unfortunately, the requisite external financing could not be arranged, resulting in the firm being closed. Prior to that, I had been with an apparel manufacturer that downsized its operations.

He should have asked himself if the negative information added anything to his sales message. Too often, job-seekers try to tell their entire career sagas in the cover letter, sparing no detail. Remember that your letter should offer a taste—an appetizer, and a good one at that. Your resume provides a little of the meal, while the interview is the place for the full banquet that is your career—including any less-than-savory aspects.

• You sound too desperate and as though you are willing to do anything. One job-seeker wrote:

Feel free to copy and distribute my resume to any other personnel who may be interested in me.

Such a statement is a turnoff for employers. They have much more respect for applicants who know exactly what they want to do and how they can make a contribution.

• You don't know enough about the company to which you're writing. A biologist included this line in his letter:

If your corporation is involved in molecular research or biological production, I encourage you to consider me for an opening.

Most employers expect applicants to know whether the company to which they're writing offers the kind of job the applicant seeks.

• You are too wimpy and passive about your past experience. Don't use such phrases as "I was taught" or "I was given the opportunity." Say "I learned" and "I took the opportunity."

The Two Worst Cover Letters We Ever Saw:

WE'RE NOT SURE what it means that both of these letters were sent to radio stations. The letter that follows arrived on shiny corrasable paper, typed in faded gray ink, complete with sexist salutation, misspellings, typos, sentence fragments, and nothing that a good cover letter should contain.

---

65 Student Drive
Harrisburg, PA 17103
717-555-2323

Radio WHRS
34532 Highway 22
Harrisburg, PA 17103

Gentlemen:

I am a recent graduate of Harrisburg College; In which I received a Bachelor of Arts Degree in Communications. And I would very much like to persue a caree in media.

I have enclosed a copy of my resume for your review. I would appreciate it very much if you would look it over to see if I meet your standards for employment with your radio station.

I would also appreciate hearing on your decision on employment with you. One thing I can promise is that I will Give 100% to my job. Since WHRS is my hometown radio station, I only want to hear thes on it.

Thank you.
Very Truly Yours,

Gilbert David King

This one was in response to a classified ad seeking an ad copywriter for a radio station. Is this guy serious? As if the letter weren't bad enough, the sample he sent bordered on pornographic.

Randy Ricci
1601 Washington St.
Tacoma, WA 98000

I am currently a paint salesman. I have previously worked as the manager of a frankfurter restaurant and as a market researcher.

I am also a writer. I've written about fifty short stories and two short novels. I read a lot and have some knowledge of current events. Enclosed is a sample from one of my novels.

I'm a creative guy. Maybe, I could be a copywriter.

Randy Ricci

Checklist

Your cover letter is ready for mailing! Or is it? Compare it to this checklist to see if you've written the most dynamic letter possible.

✔ Is it an original letter rather than a mass-produced copy?

✔ Is it addressed to a named individual? (unless it is a response to a blind ad)

✔ If it's a response to a blind ad, is the salutation nonsexist?

✔ Does the letter grab the reader's attention in the first paragraph?

✔ Is it confident without being arrogant?

✔ Have you left out everything negative?

✔ Is the letter neat and attractive?

✔ Is every word spelled correctly? Is all grammar, syntax, punctuation, and capitalization correct? Is the letter free of typographical errors?

✔ Is it no longer than one page?

✔ Is the letter concise and to the point?

✔ Does it avoid such cliches as "I have taken the liberty of sending my resume enclosed herewith"?

✔ If it's in response to an ad, does the letter speak to the requirements of the position?

✔ Is it interesting?

✔ Does it project the image of a person you would like to get to know better if you were the employer? Have you read it from the employer's perspective?

✔ Have you told the employer what you can do for him rather than what he can do for you?

✔ Have you presented your Unique Selling Proposition?

✔ If you're a recent grad, have you avoided overreliance on an academic frame of reference?

✔ Have you avoided pleading for favors?

✔ Have you avoided getting too detailed?

✔ Have you spelled out what kind of job you're looking for?

✔ Have you avoided rewriting your resume in your cover letter?

✔ Have you avoided describing your personal objectives in vague terms?

✔ Have you avoided asking for career counseling?

✔ Have you avoided listing hobbies or interests unless relevant to the position?

✔ Have you listed accomplishments?

✔ Is it clear where the employer can reach you during business hours? Have you ensured that either a person or a machine will take the employer's call?

✔ Have you used action verbs?

✔ Have you requested action, and told the employer you'll call for an appointment?

✔ Have you signed your name boldly and confidently?

The Big Picture

W E'VE POINTED OUT that your cover letter is especially important because of today's fiercely competitive job market. Seasoned professionals are out of work—sometimes for months—because corporate downsizing has eliminated their jobs. Recent college graduates are finding fewer college recruiters on their campuses and discovering that a college degree doesn't guarantee an immediate job offering.

The up side is that recent employment-outlook surveys show a strong degree of optimism. Among businesses with more than 15,000 employees, the number of companies looking to hire additional employees outnumbered those contemplating staff reductions by more than four to one. Among small businesses optimism about future economic prospects is boosting hiring plans.

To better understand how to make your cover letter work effectively in these competitive times, it is helpful to look at the big picture. The Domino Effect, Marketability, and Networking comprise the job-search big picture.

Domino Effect: If you overlook one element in your job search, the pieces will not fall into place, and you may not get the job you wanted. The five key dominos include:

- Marketing preparation.

- Your dynamic cover letter.

- Your resume, which also must be professional, and to help you develop a superb resume we've included the names of three excellent books in the "Recommended Reading" section.

- Interviewing skills.

- Follow-up. Follow up everything you do—follow up job leads, follow up your cover letters, follow up your interviews.

Marketability: The more you strive to improve your marketability, the more effective your job search will be. Keep in mind that marketing yourself to potential employers is central to the search. Employers will rarely seek you out because of *who* you are, so seek them out and present yourself in a manner that will inspire them to hire you. That's what marketing is all about—promoting a product, which in this case is you. The job search is no time to be modest; tout your accomplishments, your skills, your education. Don't be afraid to toot your horn in your cover letter. This is also not the time to be disorganized or unprepared;

develop a plan and follow through. As a starting point, test your marketability with the quiz at the end of this section.

Networking: It's one of the keys to any successful job search. Networking means developing a broad list of contacts—people you've met through various social and business functions—and using them to your advantage when you look for a job. People in your network may be able to give you job leads, offer you advice and information about a particular company or industry, and introduce you to others so that you can expand your network. The best place to start networking is with your family and friends. Talk to co-workers, colleagues in your industry, and those you meet at industry professional gatherings such as trade shows and conferences. In short, tell everyone you know you're looking for a job. It is through networking that you'll pick up names of referrals to use in your cover letters. The key to successful networking is being organized (for example, keeping a business card file) and staying in contact (for example, through regular phone calls, e-mail, and holiday greetings).

Know the Domino Effect

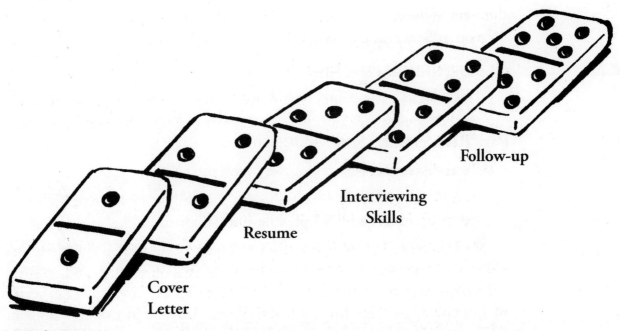

Follow-up

Interviewing
Skills

Resume

Cover
Letter

Marketing
Preparation

Test Your Marketability

Part I: Personal and Professional Development

	Yes	No
1. I read newspapers and magazines (including trade journals) regularly to stay abreast of key issues in business and my field of interest.	☑	☐
2. I have the appropriate education and experience for the kind of job I am interested in attaining.	☑	☐
3. I attend seminars and workshops that will add to my knowledge and expertise.	☐	☑
4. I belong to at least one professional organization.	☐	☑
5. I have had increasing levels of responsibility and/or been promoted in the past five years.	☑	☐

Part II: Preparation

	Yes	No
1. I have identified my key skills and abilities, as well as my strengths and weaknesses.	☑	☐
2. I know how to dress professionally.	☑	☐
3. I know the key elements (my Unique Selling Proposition) that differentiate me from other job applicants.	☑	☐
4. I know exactly the kind of job I want next.	☑	☐
5. I can research companies and industries.	☐	☑

Part III: Networking

	Yes	No
1. I keep in contact with colleagues I have met at professional events.	☑	☐
2. I keep in contact with people I have worked with in the past.	☑	☐
3. I attend professional conventions and make contacts with leaders in my field.	☐	☑
4. I introduce myself to others at social and business functions.	☑	☐
5. I exchange business cards with all new people I meet at these functions.	☑	☐

Part IV: Cover Letter Essentials

	Yes	No

1. I have developed and honed, and can communicate, my Unique Selling Proposition. ☑ ☐

2. I address all my cover letters to named individuals (except when answering blind-box classified ads). ☑ ☐

3. I never leave the ball in the potential employer's court; I always take a proactive approach. ☑ ☐

4. I tell what I can do for the company rather than what the company can do for me. ☑ ☐

5. I have eliminated all errors from my cover letters, and printed them on standard business-paper stock using a high-quality printer. ☑ ☐

Part V: Resume Necessities

1. I have identified two or three key accomplishments for each job I have had. ☑ ☐

2. I have determined my best format (chronological, functional, or some combination of the two) for my resume. ☑ ☐

3. I have used action verbs in my descriptions. ☑ ☐

4. I have eliminated all errors from my resumes and printed them on standard business-paper stock, using a high-quality printer. ☑ ☐

5. I have produced a resume that stands out from other resumes. ☑ ☐

Now total your answers.

If your "yes" answers total:

23–25	you're in great shape
20–22	you need some fine-tuning
18–20	you need more preparation
under 18	you have a lot of work ahead of you

Sources of Job Leads

YOUR NEWSPAPER, BUSINESS magazine, or trade journal contains more than just want ads to help in your job-search. (Don't forget that a company's annual report is often the best source for these same kinds of leads.) Here are other stories to look at when developing a list of contacts for your search.

• Stories about products or services in great demand. Companies with hot products may be looking to expand their work force. You may be able to get in on the ground floor by writing a dynamic cover letter to the company before they advertise for more workers.

• Your knowledge of technological breakthroughs, new patents, discoveries, and other developments in an industry or occupation can make a big impression in your letter, especially if you can catch on to the trend before anyone else does.

• Most business sections in both business/trade magazines and newspapers run a column listing promotions, retirements, and sometimes terminations and resignations. The out-going person may create an opening you could fill.

• Contract awards. When a company successfully bids on the right to manufacture goods or perform services for another company or the government, chances are the company awarded the contract will need more workers.

• Major events, such as a world's fair or Olympics in the city in which a company is located (or a company supplying such an event) create job openings.

• The opening of a new plant or facility can create opportunities.

• Reports of increased sales and earnings, which can be found not only in external publications, but also in the company's own annual report, may signal an expansion of the work force.

• Is the corporate headquarters moving to your city or state? Undoubtedly the firm will need local people to fill openings.

• Mergers and acquisitions can create opportunities because many workers leave a merged company in the face of an uncertain future.

• Stock underwritings of new and developing companies may foretell opportunities because there will now be capital available to fill openings and create new positions.

• Articles on meeting speakers and award-winners can provide fodder for dynamic cover letters.

Source: Jack Erdlen, chairman of Costello, Erdlen & Company; Wellesley, Massachusetts

New Sources of Job Leads
on the Information Superhighway

I F YOU HAVE access to a commercial online service or the Internet, the massive network of computer networks, you can dip into a wealth of resources—including not only new ways to use your cover letter, but also general tools for job-seekers.

The importance of a dynamic cover letter takes on a whole new dimension in cyberspace. After all, if you write a less than stellar cover letter on paper, an employer might not call you right away, but at least your letter could get a second chance after sitting around on a desk for awhile. If you send a letter electronically, however, all an employer has to do is press the DELETE key if your letter is not a grabber. Thus, all our credos about writing an attention-getting letter become all the more important on the information superhighway.

Job-seekers are using the superhighway more and more to send job-search correspondence. We know because we've critiqued dozens of letters online, some of which appear in the sample section at the back of the book. Most colleges offer free Internet accounts to students, and folks who aren't students can access the Internet through various commercial services, such as CompuServe, Prodigy, GEnie, and America Online.

This book can neither tell you everything you need to know about the Internet nor every online resource for job-seekers, but we offer several Internet resources that are so comprehensive that they will tell you how to find dozens more resources. The wonderful thing about the information superhighway is that once you tap into one resource, many others reveal themselves. If you have or are contemplating getting access to the Internet, you'll find literally hundreds of books available on its use. If the terminology that follows is Greek to you, you can learn what you need to know about it from one of those books. The system operator of your local network can be quite helpful, too.

Job-search resources available through Gopher: To find an astonishingly comprehensive collection of Internet resources for your job search—and a list of many, many places where you can post your cover letter and resume electronically, use the Internet tool called Gopher. Gopher is the menu-driven system for organizing information on the Internet. Gopher to una.hh.lib.umich.edu. Choose the menu item "inetdirs." From the next menu, select "All Guides." Finally, from the last menu, choose "Employment Opportunities."

Also try gophering to garnet.msen.com 9062, the Online Career Center. You can post your cover letter and resume here and search for job openings.

Lists of job-search books and other resources are also available.

A guide called Special Internet Connections, also known as the Yanoff List (after its author, Scott Yanoff) contains a section on career-search resources. Although it is available in other ways on the Internet, you can gopher it through csd4.csd.uwm.edu. From the first menu, choose "UWM's New Gopher Server." From the next menu, select "Remote Information Services." Finally, from the last menu, choose "Special Internet Connections (Yanoff List)." Page down the document until you come to Career Centers Online.

Job-search resources available through World Wide Web (WWW): World Wide Web is a hypertext-based Internet tool used for browsing Internet resources. Try this WWW site: URL:http://www.careermosaic.com. Also, you can try the WWW sites URL:http://WWW.careermag.com/careermag and URL:http://WWW.jobline.com/jobline.

Cover Letter Honor Roll: Sample Letters

I N THE FIRST edition of *Dynamic Cover Letters*, we provided samples of excellent, mediocre, and poor cover letters and gave them letter grades from A+ down to F. In this edition, *all* the samples made the honor roll. Because we discovered that readers learned more and were more inspired by the best cover letters, every sample letter is one that received an A. With identities of writers changed to protect privacy, the samples are all based on real letters. We're sure you'll find many good ideas for your own cover letters within these samples.

B. J. Johnson
250 College Heights #22
Jupiter, FL 33458
Ph # (305) 555-5487

September 9, 1994

Mr. Fred Peterson
Ford Motor Company
Dearborn, MI 48121

Dear Mr. Peterson,

My solid, hands-on experience in CAD, designing ICs and layouts, and extensive knowledge in hardware description languages (VHDL, Verilog) and analog simulation software (SPICE) would provide me with the opportunity to excel in a design capacity with your firm.

My coursework has prepared me well for a position in the Digital/Hardware/ASIC and VLSI/Architecture fields, and my research is in design and implementation of Broadband crosspoint switching fabric. I am well aware that your company does high-quality work in these areas.

My previous employers can attest that I am not only organized and detail-oriented, but I also work well under pressure and on deadline. I work well with a variety of people.

I am immediately available for employment and am prepared to relocate either domestically or overseas.

I believe my qualifications are an excellent fit with the needs of your company and that it would be worthwhile for us to meet. I will contact you in ten days to schedule an interview. Should you wish to contact me before that time, you may reach me during business hours at 305-555-5487. Thank you for your time and consideration.

Sincerely,

B. J. Johnson

Glennis Cook
3335 NW 39th Terrace
Gainesville, FL 32606
(904) 555-1009

February 9, 1994

Mrs. Rita Williams
The Limited, Inc.
P.O. Box 16000
Columbus, OH 43216-6000

Dear Mrs. Williams:

Having been employed previously by The Limited, I know firsthand that your corporation is a strong and growing institution in which I could make a valuable contribution using management and marketing experience garnered through both education and experience.

My solid educational background coupled with retail experience can only profit your corporation. That's why I'm writing to arrange an interview when your campus recruiter visits the University of Florida on April 10. I understand you will be recruiting a manager for your Lerner's West Palm Beach, Florida, store, as well as for a manager for your Victoria's Secret Clearwater, Florida, store.

My experience in other retail outlets has broadened my perspective and provided me with a strong customer-service orientation. I possess a clear understanding of inventory-control procedures and am adept with many computer programs used in the retail field.

Mrs. Williams, although I certainly want to meet with your recruiter when he or she comes to my campus, I would also be willing to interview for this position before that time. I'll give you a call next week to see which route you feel is preferable. If you'd like to contact me, my number is (904) 555-1009.

Thanks so much for considering me.

Sincerely,

Glennis Cook

Gary Frey
5465 Ferguson Avenue
Pittsburgh, PA 15213
412-555-4349

September 19, 1994

Anne Mach
Director, Human Resources
3M Corporation
St. Paul, MN 09631

Dear Ms. Mach:

My technical background, demonstrated leadership skills, and ability to meet the needs of the customer would enable me to make a valuable contribution in a chemical-engineering position at 3M Corporation. Thus, I am writing to request a meeting with your campus recruiter when he/she visits Carnegie Mellon University on Oct. 20. I will graduate from the Carnegie Institute of Technology at Carnegie Mellon University with a B.S. in chemical engineering in May 1995.

My current position as community adviser, the senior-most position in the residence-life office, with 248 people under my direct or indirect supervision, demonstrates my leadership ability. Previous employers can tell you that, because I am highly independent and responsible and because I enjoy dealing with people, I have consistently been promoted to levels of greater responsibility.

My ability to function as both a leader and a team player would enable me to serve the company well in a project-management capacity. My professors can confirm that I have acted as a team player in many academic work-group situations. In design and lab courses, my roles as leader and team member have involved collaboration, delegation of work, scheduling deadlines and meeting them, making group decisions, and sharing the leadership role. I am well experienced in gauging and improving group dynamics.

My challenging and competitive academic program has included such unique courses as photochemistry, process controls, process engineering and design, and unit operations laboratory, all of which would be particularly useful in the chemical-engineering area, particularly in project management.

Ms. Mach, I will call you the week of October 10 to arrange an appointment with your campus recruiter. In the meantime, I would appreciate receiving additional information on employment opportunities and a job application form. Thanks very much for your consideration.

Very truly yours,

Gary Frey

55 Davis Hall
University Park, PA 16802
(814) 555-8729

September 24, 1994

Mr. Van Thorne
Director of Programming
Westinghouse Electric
Pittsburgh, PA 15222

Dear Mr. Thorne:

Your employee, Jennifer Fiester, suggested I contact you about a programming position with Westinghouse. As a senior student expecting a Bachelor of Science degree in Computer Science from Pennsylvania State University, I am ready to make a meaningful contribution to the Westinghouse team.

Both my academic career and employment experience have prepared me well for a career in programming. I have been trained in developing, designing, integrating, and documenting various application programs, and programming using IBM Mainframe and UNIX operating systems. The many programming classes I've taken have taught me several different programming languages, including C, FORTRAN, Pascal, COBOL, Assembly, and Standard ML.

My previous employers can affirm that they have entrusted me with major responsibilities and that I have adapted quickly to each of my positions. For example, as head manager at Sam's Food Market last summer, I exclusively managed the store, delegated work for employees, and handled daily cash flow.

In addition, my position as a social director for my club at the university has helped me further enhance my communication skills.

Because you undoubtedly realize that a letter and resume can convey only a limited sense of a person's qualifications, I believe it would be productive for us to meet in person so I can explain my credentials more fully.

I will contact you in ten days to arrange a meeting. Should you wish to reach me before that, my number is (814) 555-8729. Please leave a message if I am not available. I look forward to meeting with you. Thank you for your time and consideration.

Sincerely yours,

Sunny Harrison

Kurt Mayer
65443 Providence Blvd.
#96
Detroit, MI 48207
313-555-5621

September 6, 1994

Mr. Joseph Oliker
Human Resource Department
Whirlpool, Inc.
Benton Harbor, MI 49022

Dear Mr. Oliker:

Having worked in service-based organizations, I know how valuable good employees are. All organizations, after all, have access to the same information, the same suppliers, and the same consumers. The organization that differentiates itself through effective recruiting, retention, training, and managing its people is the best equipped to succeed in today's competitive business environment.

My desire to contribute to a company's competitive edge has motivated me to study organizational psychology as an undergraduate student and pursue an MBA focusing on human-resource management. I would like to put my knowledge and experience to work for you.

The financial, managerial, program development and leadership skills I gained through both employment and extracurricular experience would enable me to make a significant contribution to your organization's success. My previous employers and professors can verify that these skills, combined with my coursework, motivation, and determination to succeed, will make me a valuable asset to your organization.

I would like to have the opportunity to meet with you and discuss how I might enhance your company's continued success. I will contact you the week of September 20 to arrange a meeting. Should you wish to reach me in the meantime, you may call me at 313-555-5621. I appreciate your time and consideration.

Sincerely,

Kurt Mayer

Nell Bannister
2364 South Woodland Blvd.
DeLand, FL 32720
(904) 555-5531

May 3, 1994

Ms. Jane Sutherland
First Union
One First Union Court
Charlotte, NC 28288

Dear Ms. Sutherland:

My training in marketing and experience in the banking industry parallels the requirements of First Union's Consumer Banker Associate Program. I have recently graduated from Florida State University, and I am eager to put my education to work in banking.

The experience I gained in my summer jobs in banking would be a genuine asset to First Union. In the Barnett Merchant Services Department, I learned valuable communication skills and a professional attitude. As a loan processor for Banc Boston Mortgage Company, I took the opportunity to learn how loans are processed and how relationships between agents are established and maintained. I also developed problem-solving and decision-making skills; by the end of the summer, I worked in the cash-claims analysis department making loan-foreclosure decisions.

Having worked as a computer-lab assistant while putting myself through college, I also have well-developed computer skills and a familiarity with many of the most popular software programs.

Ms. Sutherland, I believe it would be worthwhile for us to meet. I will give your secretary a call Wednesday, May 18, to schedule an appointment. Should you have any questions about my interests or qualifications in the meantime, please feel free to call me at (904) 555-5531.

I thank you for considering me for the Consumer Banker Associate Program and look forward to meeting with you.

Sincerely,

Nell Bannister

1038 Glenwood Path
Tallahassee, FL 32308
U.S.A.
(904) 555-3211

February 27, 1994

Torsten Jonsson
Personalavd
SAS
161 87 Stockholm
Sweden

Dear Mr. Jonsson:

My education and experience in marketing and international business, as well as my fluency in English, Spanish and Italian, would enable me to contribute significantly to a global accounts position with Swedish Airlines. I would be interested in employment anywhere in the world.

I will graduate this May with a Bachelor of Science in Marketing from Florida State University, where I was president of the International Business Society. I demonstrated solid skills in marketing research and promotion during my experience at the Bureau of International Trade and Development at the Florida Department of Commerce, which would enable me to sell the airline's services worldwide. I also developed considerable facility with computers.

As a member of the family of a U.S. Foreign Service Diplomat, I have acquired a unique view of the international business scene, numerous cross-cultural skills, and adaptability. I am well traveled and have lived in a wide variety of international locales.

I am eager to advance the success of your company, and I believe it would be advantageous to set up a meeting with your American human-resources representative. I plan to contact the American office in two weeks to arrange such a meeting. Should you desire to contact me in the meantime, I can be reached at (904) 555-3211.

Thank you for your consideration.

Sincerely,

Paul D. Koblenzer

Isabel Loprieno
485 Oak Lane
Tequesta, FL 33469
(407) 555-2435

March 27, 1994

Mr. Jerry Proboski
Federated Insurance Company
1890 Semoran Blvd., Suite 273
Winter Park, FL 32792

Dear Mr. Proboski:

Dr. Randall Scott of Stetson University suggested I contact you regarding the position you and he discussed in the Insurance Trainee Program of Federated Insurance Company.

I am a May 1994 graduate, but I am not a typical new graduate. I put myself through school by selling radio advertising and serving in a customer-service capacity in an art gallery. All my jobs during my college years enhanced my formal education and provided considerable practical experience in sales and marketing that would enable me to make a real impact as a trainee with Federated. I also participated in a number of university-sponsored marketing research projects.

As Dr. Scott can verify, my education and practical experience, coupled with my maturity and marketing skills, will be an asset to your firm.

I am enthusiastic about a career in insurance and am willing to relocate for your training program.

I will follow up this letter with a phone call next week.

Thank you for your consideration.

Sincerely,

Isabel Loprieno

Recent Grad Letter

✔ Demonstrates knowledge of company
✔ Makes effective connection between retail-sales experience and outside-sales career goal

Heather Barker
2838 E. Michigan Avenue
DeLand, FL 32720
(904) 555-2872

March 11, 1994

Dr. Jill Fenimore
Director of Pharmaceutical Sales
Schering-Plough, Inc.
Madison, NJ 07940

Dear Dr. Fenimore,

Since I work in the pharmacy field, I am aware of your company's reputation in pharmaceutical research and sales. My solid background in the retail pharmacy business, along with the skills and experience that accompanied my education, should be of interest to you. My ability to communicate well with physicians and pharmacies in selling pharmaceuticals would allow me to make a difference at Schering-Plough.

I will receive a Bachelor of Business Administration in marketing from Stetson University in May 1995. Throughout my academic career, I have cultivated my special interest in pharmaceutical sales through my studies of professional selling. I would now like to draw on those abilities as a professional in the field.

I am confident that my knowledge and abilities would be of value to your company. I would like to request a few minutes of your time to discuss my qualifications. I will contact you on March 27 to arrange a meeting. If you have any questions in the meantime, please do not hesitate to call.

Thank you for your time and consideration.

Sincerely,

Heather Barker

Chris Barton
2104 Pinhorn Drive
Bridgewater, NJ 08807
(908) 555-9208

October 1, 1994

Ms. Sharron Cody
Director of Human Resources
Sak's Fifth Avenue
500 Fifth Avenue
New York, NY 10022

Dear Ms. Cody:

I'm writing to follow up on a phone conversation you had with Rutgers University Assistant Director of Career Services Dawn DeLoach about the retail management-trainee position you expect to have available in May 1995. I've developed a strong foundation in retail, I am highly customer-service oriented, and I stand poised to bring my skills to your fine organization.

My retail experience includes an internship with your Short Hills store, as well as summer and seasonal positions with various specialty stores and boutiques.

I've also developed my abilities to lead and influence people through a long record of activities at my university. Combined with my major coursework in marketing, my secondary focus in communications has enabled me to hone my skills in interacting productively with people.

I am convinced that I am particularly well suited to meet the challenges of this position and to provide top performance in retail management. At your convenience, I would like to arrange a time for a personal interview, and I will call you in ten days to set up such a meeting. Should you wish to reach me before then, please call (908) 555-9208.

Thank you for your time and consideration.

Sincerely,

Chris Barton

Jason Jay Johnson
108 North Lincoln Blvd.
Omaha, NE 68132
402-555-7154

Oct. 1, 1994

Mr. Gavin Nehemiah
Omaha Snow Devils
400 E. Icy Lane
Omaha, NE 68130

Dear Mr. Nehemiah:

Dr. Patrick Oliphant suggested I write to you about your opening in the advertising and promotion department with the Omaha Snow Devils.

As an experienced athlete and a marketing major, I have played a major role in numerous fund-raisers. I also hold a part-time position as a customer-service assistant in a supermarket while pursuing my degree and playing on the college baseball team. I've also worked as an assistant coach for summer baseball clinics held on my campus.

My interest and skills in sports marketing are a good match with the requirements of the position you have open.

I believe we should meet to discuss how I might contribute to the team's visibility and box-office success. I'd like to phone you during the week of Oct. 18 to arrange such a meeting. You may also contact me at 402-555-7154.

Thank you, Mr. Nehemiah, for appraising my candidacy for this position.

Very truly yours,

Jason Jay Johnson

✔ The applicant is writing to a manager who hired him for what turned out to be a lengthy series of summer jobs and internships. The manager has now moved on to another company, so the applicant is writing to her to ask her to consider hiring him again.

John Hood
906 S. Dixie Avenue, #20
Leesburg, FL 32748
(407) 555-8225

May 1, 1994

Ms. Debbie Cooper
Vice President of Marketing
Home Shopping Network, Inc.
St. Petersburg, FL 33710

Dear Ms. Cooper:

Six years ago when you hired me for my first job, I wonder if you realized that the work would become a career. Since those early days, I have advanced with Pass, Forte & Blacker to work in the departments of Catalog Control and Creative Marketing.

From this experience, I have become an expert on the intricacies of nonstore retailing. I helped spearhead a computer tracking system that allowed us to develop a relationship marketing program that, in only the first two years of operation, has increased sales by 35 percent. Furthermore, I have solid sales experience, as well as logistics experience. I know I can apply these skills at Home Shopping and help continue HSN's strong sales gains.

I want to thank you for giving me that first opportunity to explore retail, not only because I enjoy the work so much but because I've learned enough to know that I want to make a long-term commitment to this field. I have built on my retail experience with market-research consultation work.

Ms. Cooper, it was such a pleasure to work with you in the past; I look forward to the opportunity to do so again. I'd like to meet with you to discuss the possibilities, and I'll call you soon to set up such a meeting. I can be reached at (407) 555-8225.

Thanks again for the career boost and for considering me a second time.

Sincerely,

John Hood

Mercedes Moser
600 Rolling Acres Road
Stonybrook, NY 11790
(516) 555-2236

April 5, 1994

Mr. Lloyd Langford
United Technologies, Inc.
Hartford, CT 06103

Dear Mr. Langford,

Could you use a scientist or field technician who gained experience on the successful operation of a large-scale (annual budget of $2 million) bioremediation project while still a college undergraduate? I am just such a scientist, and I would like to enhance the success of an environmental services firm such as United Technologies.

I hold a Sc.B. in Environmental Science from Yale University, where my academic focus was in biology and chemistry. I utilized the knowledge gained from my coursework to complete a one-year thesis on heavy-metal sequestration in a biological waste-water treatment plant. Not only did I refine my skills at working independently, but I also learned how to effectively communicate with and obtain information from colleagues working in my area of research. My thesis and course work provided significant exposure to experimental design techniques, statistics, and proper laboratory procedure.

My familiarity with the XRF eventually led to various projects with both a senior geology professor and the director of Yale's Department of Environmental Studies. I am confident of my ability to successfully complete the tasks with which I would be confronted at United Technologies.

Although I am interested in gaining exposure to all types of remediation technologies, I am particularly enthusiastic about working on projects that involve bioremediation. Having studied this subject extensively, I have become knowledgeable with a variety of biotreatment techniques, including: landfarming, liquid/solids treatment, submerged fixed-film bioreactors (growth- and decay-mode), and PACT.

I know that your corporation seeks motivated, responsible individuals, and I would very much like to meet with you to discuss my possible employment. Please permit me to phone you late next week for an appointment. Meanwhile, please feel free to contact me at (516) 555-2236. Thanking you for your consideration, I look forward to meeting with you soon.

Sincerely,

Mercedes Moser

Katlynn P. Morgan
1540 Republic Drive
Orlando, FL 32819
(407) 555-4947

Ms. Rachelle Larson
Cellular One
501 E. Kennedy Blvd.
Tampa, FL 33602

Dear Rachelle,

It certainly was a pleasure to speak with you recently. You'll find that my proven track record in sales and marketing makes me the ideal candidate for the sales position we discussed in your regional sales office in Tampa.

I was a first-place winner in personal selling at the DECA National Convention in 1990. I have continued this record of excellence in my college career with a recent national award from the American Marketing Association. I believe my proficient oral and written skills, as well as my natural ability to work well as a team player, makes me a valuable and productive employee.

I am a well-rounded student, as you will notice on my resume. I have both participated and held leadership positions in various extracurricular activities. I am a hard worker, and my enthusiastic personality and positive attitude make me an excellent co-worker.

I am convinced that you will find my qualifications strong enough to justify an interview to explore mutual interests. I will be calling you in a week or so. Should you need any additional information, please contact me. Again, Rachelle, thanks for your consideration.

Sincerely,

Katlynn P. Morgan

287 21st Street
Irvington, NJ 07111
(201) 555-2132

October 17, 1994

English as a Second Language Coordinator
Essex County School Board
380 Main Street
Newark, NJ 07070

Dear Coordinator:

As a student in the Teaching English to Speakers of Other Languages program at SUNY Stonybrook, I seek a school district where I can have an impact, as I do my student teaching in the spring semester of 1995. As a student teacher, I will give as much to my students and master teacher as I will learn from them.

I have four years experience working as a teaching assistant in the Sussex County school system at all grade levels during the summer and university holidays. I have substituted in many different schools, including an alternative high school for students at risk of dropping out of school and those with drug and alcohol problems, and the adolescent psychiatric ward of a hospital. I believe these experiences in difficult situations have given me the stamina to be an effective teacher under various conditions.

In addition to completing all the courses required by the university and the state for KP12 TESOL certification, I have taken two semesters of ESL teaching practicum and a class in methods of teaching foreign languages. My required and elective course work combined with my experience have prepared me to be an effective teacher, and I believe that I am better prepared than many other student teachers.

My next step in preparing to be a teacher is student teaching. I am interested in experiencing both elementary and high school settings. Instead of teaching at an elementary school for a month and then moving on to the high school, I would ideally like to spend part of each day at each school because I believe it is important to make a long-term commitment to my students.

I'd like to meet with you to discuss the ESL student-teaching positions that are available in your district. I will stop by your booth at the teacher-recruitment fair next month to set up a meeting. If you need to reach me in the meantime, please call (201) 555-2132.

Sincerely,

Dexter Mulkey

Cody Barbara Bucher
108 Hilltop Way
Redwood City, CA 94062
415-555-2891

March 2, 1994

Mr. Steve Davis,
Sales Manager
Sutter Home Winery, Inc.
Napa, CA 94589

Dear Mr. Davis,

Much of the money I earned while in junior high school, high school, and college has come from sales, and I would like to continue pursuing my interest in marketing and sales with a summer internship in the field. I am writing to ask if Sutter Home has any positions available to college students during the summer months.

This year, as a freshman at the University of California at San Francisco, I became a sales person for our student newspaper, which is published twice a week. At the start of the second semester, I was promoted to Sales Manager, a position that gives me the responsibility for all the advertising for one issue a week. We do all of our own production, so in addition to servicing existing clients and attracting new clients, I have become skilled at layout techniques.

During my senior year at Redwood City High, I raised more than $2,000 so that my class could travel to Los Angeles and help earthquake victims. In that same year, through my after school position with Artists Supplies, Inc., I was able to save more than $10,000 for my college career.

I would like to emphasize that I am looking for experience in sales management and marketing this summer — salary is not my primary concern. I would greatly appreciate any position that you could offer. I will be available during Spring Break, from March 13–20, and I would like to meet that week. I will call you early next week to set up an appointment.

Thanks so much for your time and consideration.

Sincerely,

Cody Barbara Bucher

PO Box 134
Piscataway, NJ 08855-1119
(609) 555-2922

March 22, 1994

Mr. James Julia
VP, Human Resources
Allied Signal
Morris Township, NJ 07962

Dear Mr. Julia,

As a Rutgers engineering student in my junior year studying electrical engineering, I am seeking a summer internship in the Central New Jersey region in which I can make a real contribution.

My experience in retail electronics, as well as my desire to pursue research and development, have convinced me that electrical manufacturing is an option I would like to explore.

More importantly, an internship with Allied Signal would be mutually beneficial. Your company has an excellent reputation for quality, and I know that the combination of my experience, education, and motivation to excel will make me an asset for any department where you place me.

I believe it would be worthwhile for us to meet. I will contact you within a week to arrange a meeting. Should you have any questions before that time, you may reach me during business hours at 609-555-3000, or at my home number listed above.

Sincerely,

Sandy Taffida

Letter to a College Placement Office

✔ An excellent way to network

June 5, 1994

Ms. Barbara Bluebonnet
Placement Office
University of Texas
Austin, TX 78712

Dear Ms. Bluebonnet,

    I am a recent graduate of the University of Texas and am in the job market for a position in nursing. My speciality is in pediatric nursing.

    I am hoping that you will keep my file current and inform me when any nursing recruiters are on campus for interviews or when you hear of openings in my field.

    Enclosed is an updated version of my resume for your files. Also please note my new address and telephone number for your records.

    Thank you so much for your help.

Sincerely,

Alisa Baxter

Libby Samuels
238A Cloudy Sky Drive
Seattle, WA 98103
(206) 555-3728

September 15, 1994

Ms. Jill Sabovsky
Filenet Corporation
3565 Harbor Blvd.

Costa Mesa, CA 92626-1420

Dear Ms. Sabovsky,

Your colleague Jack Southerly and I have been talking about how my skills might fit at Filenet Corporation. He said he'd discussed with you the possibility that I might assist you with some projects, so I wanted to introduce myself, and tell you a little of what I've done since working with Jack at InfoSource.

I got my master's degree at Antioch University, Seattle, in whole systems design for organizational change. Since then I've been doing consulting for organizations on a variety of planned change projects. While working for InfoSource, I designed and facilitated a series of goal-setting and evaluation meetings to implement their gain-share plan. I have worked with the local YWCA to design and conduct board planning retreats, and I facilitated a series of sessions for Smith Barney Shearson to develop their company mission statement.

The applicable skills in all of these projects are the ability to lead groups in effective work sessions, to design processes that accomplish the appropriate tasks, and to communicate in a way that draws out the group's combined knowledge.

I'm looking for a position where my talents could be fully engaged. Jack made it clear that the decision for an assistant is yours, and that any position would have to go through the normal posting process. I simply wanted to let you know I'm eager, and hope to find a fit at Filenet Corporation.

I will be arriving in Costa Mesa around the second week in October. I don't yet know my local number or address. If you don't get an opportunity to call me before September 30th, I'll get in touch on my arrival. Thanks for your consideration.

Sincerely,

Libby Samuels

Referral Letter

✔ Note positive, confident tone

Mark R. Shaw
1545 Elmont Street
Kansas City, MO 64114
(816) 555-3829

November 30, 1994

Mr. C. Benjamin Cornfield
Human Resources Dept.
Sprint
Kansas City, MO 64100

Dear Mr. Cornfield,

Nanette Newell tells me that you are looking for a motivated employee for the job of Customer Service Representative. I know I have the background and the personality to excel in this position.

I have extensive, high-energy customer-service experience, and I desire to make customer service my life's work. I have frequently called upon my ability to communicate effectively, handle customer problems quickly and personably, and succeed in high-stress situations.

In addition, I have excellent organizational and writing skills, as my former employers can describe. I am currently training to enhance my IBM computer skills, and I have the desire and competence to learn quickly.

I know you won't regret giving me an opportunity to show you what I can do. I am very interested in working for your company, and I believe you will be happy with my performance.

I will call you in a few days to explore what the next steps will be.

Sincerely,

Mark R. Shaw

2114 Galloway Drive
Manhattan, Kansas 66502
(913) 555-3743

June 23, 1994

Mr. William J. Douglas
Personnel Manager
West Educational Publishing
620 Opperman Drive
St. Paul, MN 55164-0779

Dear Mr. Douglas,

Our mutual acquaintance, Dr. Dorothy Grecie, with whom I am working as a postdoctoral research associate in the department of Management Science, suggested I contact you to describe the contribution I might make in research and development or product/process development at your organization.

I have a strong background in engineering and mathematics at the undergraduate level and at the graduate level. The skills in management science attained through course work, research projects, teaching experience, and pilot plant experience would enable me to analyze ecosystems and develop new ecology-friendly products.

In addition to my research experience, I coauthored two successful grant proposals resulting from my Ph.D. research.

With my background in management engineering and science, and research experience, I am confident of my ability to meet your requirements.

Please review my qualifications and see if you agree that we should meet personally. I will call you during the week of July 10 to arrange a meeting. If you desire any additional information, I can be reached at (913) 555-3743.

Thank you for considering my qualifications.

Sincerely,

Sally Radellio

1245 University Blvd.
Tallahassee FL 32308
(904) 555-0790

20 February 1994

Mr. Morris Fiondella
Fiondella & Associates
908 Adelphi Lane
Austin, TX 78727-4111

Dear Mr. Fiondella:

I very much enjoyed meeting both you and Pete Avery at the Performance Summit '94 in Tampa. Congratulations on your selection as Production Coordinator/Manager of the Year for your work with Mariah Carey.

My experience as a production assistant, my proven organizational skills, and my flexibility to travel would all be solid assets in a tour-production position with Fiondella & Associates.

I am thoroughly familiar with the operation of concert halls through numerous part-time and volunteer production-assistant positions in which I worked on concerts featuring M.C. Hammer, New Kids on the Block, Jimmy Buffet, as well as for the Jacksonville Jazz Festival.

I have also honed my organizational skills and ability to adapt to a variety of management styles during two years as an administrative assistant.

I am widely traveled, both in the United States and abroad, and I work well on the go.

My previous employers can vouch for my ability to organize, coordinate, and make things happen. I have enclosed a list of references. I'm sure we could both benefit from another face-to-face meeting in which I would further describe my potential contribution in a tour-support position. I will call your office during the week of February 25.

Thank you for your time and consideration.

Sincerely,

Colleen Bucholtz

Jill Edwards
233 West 99th Terrace
Kansas City, MO 64114
(816) 555-2231

November 22, 1994

Continuing Education
ATTN: Sean Dunstan
College Court Building
Manhattan, Kansas 66502

Mr. Dunstan:

I am writing, in accordance with our telephone conversation of November 19, to reinforce to you how well my background aligns with the graduate-assistant position you have open for a nontraditional student coordinator.

As a former nontraditional undergraduate here at K-State, I understand the problems and frustrations of those students coming back to school after a delay—especially those who are unable to attend directly on campus. Also, as a lifelong Midwest resident, I am familiar with the vagaries of the local environment that can affect a person's ability to attend college in a traditional or regular manner.

For these reasons, I believe I am eminently qualified for the position as described. I'd like to phone you in the near future to arrange a time to discuss the good ideas I could bring to this position. Thank you very much for your time.

Sincerely,

Jill Edwards

382 E. 22 Street
New York, NY 10020
(212) 555-8928

January 23, 1994

Mr. Paul Johnson
Fashion Interiors, Inc.
32 Beacon Street
Boston, MA 02116

Dear Mr. Johnson:

I very much enjoyed talking with you last Tuesday about your need to fill your firm's architectural and interior-designer position. My seven years of experience as associate-in-charge of the interiors group at a New York architectural firm and as an architectural designer qualify me well for this position.

In my most recent position, I headed up activities ranging from complete coordination and production of construction drawings to furniture inventories, from finish and furniture selections to space planning and design development. I met with clients, identified their needs, and executed their space plans in tenant fit-outs in New York and Philadelphia. As my previous employer can attest, my work was accurate and detail oriented.

I've been extremely impressed with the fine work Fashion Interiors does, and I'm convinced that I can enhance the firm's success.

Mr. Johnson, I believe my qualifications are an excellent fit with the position, and it would be mutually beneficial for us to meet. I will call you early next week to set up an appointment for an interview.

Sincerely,

Matthew Pinch

Mary H. Hansen
2829 Woody Place
Tallahassee, FL 32308

Dr. Brett Steele
Mitchell Advertising, Inc.
2189 N. Monroe Street
Tallahassee, FL 32308

June 9, 1993

Dear Dr. Steele,

Back in January before I located to Tallahassee from Ohio, I wrote to you about the possibility of employment with your agency. You wrote me back an extremely nice letter. You said that with my qualifications, I should have no difficulty finding a job here.

I'm happy to say you were right. I'm working as the publications coordinator in the communications office of the Department of Public Works.

Having felt such a nice rapport from you in your very warm letter, I thought you might like to know that I'm here in Tallahassee and am enhancing my ability to make a contribution to an agency such as yours.

In addition to the twenty outstanding brochures I've developed so far, I've written some press releases and articles I'm pretty proud of, and I'm currently organizing press coverage for the Commissioner's upcoming trip to Mexico.

I also recently learned that the newsletter I produced in my last job won first place in a regional newsletter competition for nonprofit agencies.

I am still very interested in meeting with you. I'll give you a call in the near future to see if we can set something up. Should you wish to reach me before hearing from me, you may call me at 555-2513 during business hours.

Thank you for your consideration, and thanks again for your wonderful letter in January.

Cordially,

Mary H. Hansen

Gabriel Meenan
187 Salem Road
Tewsbury, MA 01876
(414) 555-2010

May 15, 1994

Ms. Mary Jane Collins
Senator Jack Frost Headquarters
293 Main Street
Boston, MA 02116

Dear Mary Jane,

It was truly delightful to meet you at Senator Frost's brunch on Saturday. Your sense of humor is infectious, and I'm sure it goes a long way in helping you cope with your massive workload.

I'd like to help make your work load and that of your staff lighter. You mentioned at the brunch that the time has come to hire a communications director. I'm convinced I could make a significant contribution in that position.

I have been communications director for the Institute for the Reinvention of Education for two years. I help advance the organization's agenda by developing dynamic campaigns, including one that won an "Award of Distinction" from the Massachusetts Public Relations Association.

Obviously, I am well-versed in cutting-edge education issues. But having worked as a Public Information Director at the Nebraska Association of Social Workers, I am also highly knowledgeable in many other areas in which Senator Frost is taking the lead: infant mortality, prenatal care, teen-pregnancy prevention, health care.

Mary Jane, I have enclosed some of my favorite campaign materials. I believe it would be constructive for us to meet again. I would like to be considered for the communications director position — I'm convinced my qualifications and your needs are a perfect fit.

I'll check in with you at the teacher's union luncheon next week. You may also wish to reach me. During business hours, call 555-4800 (or leave a message on my voice-message system) or leave a message on my home machine at 555-2010.

Mary Jane, thanks so much for your consideration. I look forward to talking with you again soon.

Cordially,

Gabriel Meenan

John A. Pescatello
35 W. Colgate Circle
Great Neck, NY 11021
914-555-2887

August 9, 1994

Mr. Richard McPherson
Executive Editor
Rochester News Leader
Rochester, NY 14610

Dear Dick,

I'm hoping you remember me. I worked for you as a copy editor two years ago but cut my employment there short to finish my bachelor's degree at Syracuse University. I have just learned that your arts writer is no longer with you. I'm writing to ask you to consider hiring me to replace her.

I finished my degree in humanities, an interdisciplinary degree that combines literature, art, and music. For the past year, I've worked in Syracuse University's art gallery, where I've learned and written a great deal about art.

I've written extensively about the arts both during my academic career and while working in the gallery; I've also written lots of other features and have a large portfolio I'd love to share with you. Story ideas are a particular strength; I'll bring twenty story ideas about the arts to our interview, if you agree it's worthwhile for us to talk.

I am also very conscious of the strong commitment to the arts by the publisher's family, and I believe I can do justice to their commitment by setting a high standard of excellence in arts writing at the News Leader. I'll also be a cordial representative of the paper to the arts community.

I hope you agree it would be rewarding to meet again. Knowing that you must be eager to fill the arts-writer position, I'll call to arrange a visit to your office in the next few days. Should you wish to reach me, you may call me during business hours at (914) 555-7506 or at home at (914) 555-2887.

Thank you for your consideration of me. I look forward to meeting with you again.

Cordially,

John A. Pescatello

Sarah Cornett Dinsher
1545 Willowtree Lane,
Apt. B5
Ann Arbor, MI 48105
(313) 555-7887
email:sdinsh@eecs.umich.edu

October 13th 1994

Ms. Lisa Kessler
J.P. Morgan & Co
23 Wall Street
NY, NY 10260-0023

Dear Ms. Kessler,

It was a pleasure to meet you at the Career Fair at the University of Michigan on September 26th.

I am a graduate student pursuing my M.S. degree in Electrical Engineering at the University of Michigan, and I expect to graduate in December, '94. I am majoring in Signal Processing and am particularly interested in the position of Technology Analyst at your organization.

I possess a comprehensive background in statistical signal processing, regression analysis of time-series data, parametric and non-parametric data-modeling techniques and fairly strong programming skills with 'C' and the Unix environment, as well as the necessary analytical and interpersonal skills required for a challenging position at J.P. Morgan and Co.

While my resume details my qualifications, I also wish to add that I am a quick learner and confident in my ability to meet your expectations in all spheres. My professors can back me up on these points.

If, after reviewing my resume, you agree that I may be able to contribute to your organization's goals, I would appreciate the opportunity to meet you personally. I'll phone you in two weeks to make an appointment.

Thank you for your consideration.

Sincerely,

Sarah Cornett Dinsher

Dan Bolding
233 K Street
Washington, D.C. 20520
202-555-4812

March 3, 1994

Mr. Sinclair Martin
Honcho-Search, Inc.
500 Pennsylvania Avenue
Washington, D.C. 20520

Dear Mr. Martin,

Several associates have mentioned the quality of your search work for managers in this area. Clair Taylor was particularly complimentary. I think we should get to know one another.

My experience and track record in sales and marketing have been excellent. Here's a brief summary:

- I was promoted to national sales manager after only two years with Art International and effected a 10 percent increase in market share for all products, up to 20 percent for several products. My sales force was revitalized and motivated.

- I increased the profitability by reducing costly administrative procedures. By giving the sales people more authority, time-consuming tasks were removed from their agenda and they were able to do what they do best—sell.

- My track record with all the companies I have been with from salesman to national sales manager are all positive—all have shown increased sales.

- My career has been good but our president has reluctantly agreed with me that to optimize my career possibilities, I should look to a larger organization.

Since I am quite interested in the services you have to offer, I will call you the week of March 10th. Feel free to call me at 555-4812 if you wish to speak with me earlier.

Sincerely,

Dan Bolding

Hilary Granola
2090 NE Indian Hill Lane
Beaverton, OR 97005
(503) 555-4562

June 30, 1994

Satya Ramidipati
Oregon Biotechnology Association
111 SW Columbia Avenue
Portland, OR 97201

Dear Ms. Ramidipati,

I have learned that your organization is committed to matching the biotech/pharmaceutical openings in member companies with quality applicants. Thus, I am writing to introduce you to a background that should be of great interest to your member firms and to ask your assistance in my quest for a research position.

My education has been in Chemical Engineering, while my research training and interests are in Molecular and Cellular Biology.

For the past four years I have been working on my Ph.D. thesis, which concerns secretion of foreign proteins from yeast. I am developing a vector system that allows the gene for a foreign protein to be integrated into the chromosomes of yeast.

This research is directly applicable to the production of pharmaceuticals as well as being of basic interest in identifying the key factors of secretion. In the process, I have developed advanced molecular biological lab skills and have been able to apply my engineering expertise to the project.

I am quite flexible on geographic location and have focused my attention upon finding a company where my skills can be fully utilized and a research position where I can make a lasting and profit-making contribution.

If you can be of any assistance in identifying a company that may have need of a research scientist with my skills and interests, please don't hesitate to give them a copy of my enclosed resume and extend them an invitation to contact me. In the meantime, I'd like to contact you to brainstorm career strategies with you.

Thank you for your time and assistance.

Sincerely,

Hilary Granola

Matthew Pinelas
32 Longleaf Lane
Portland, ME 04105
(207) 555-3832

July 23, 1994

Ms. Stephanie Thomas
Quality Systems Director
Sara Lee, Inc.
Chicago, IL 60602

Dear Ms. Thomas,

During my graduate studies, I learned that Sara Lee is a highly respected organization and well-known for its concern for quality and safety. My ability to analyze food systems in terms of equipment, processing, quality, and microbial safety parallels your company's commitment.

The value that I can add to your organization based on more than six years' worth of accomplishments is summarized below:

• Outstanding written and verbal communication skills that would enable me to write reports and interact with other team members.

• Well-developed analytical and quantitative skills that would allow me to review food systems and processes with precision.

• A unique combination of science and engineering skills developed through course work and research projects.

After you review my qualifications, I would welcome the opportunity to speak with you personally. I will call you during the week of August 7th to ensure that you have received my resume and to answer any questions you might have. If you desire any additional information, I can be reached at (207) 555-3832. Thank you for considering my qualifications.

Sincerely,

Matthew Pinelas

12 September, 1994

Response to your Internet
posting for position number
TS0008

Dear Friends:

My fifteen years of diverse experience in the computer field make me exactly the kind of value-added employee you need in the position you are advertising.

As a Senior Systems Analyst for the Greater Boston United Way and an independent consultant helping clients select, install and implement PC solutions, my accomplishments to date include:

- installing and administering Novell, Windows for Workgroups, 3Com, and LANtastic local area networks;

- integrating the LANs with a Wang VS 7120;

- connecting the Archdiocese to the Internet;

- developing, documenting & implementing various database applications;

- installing and administering all aspects of the Computron general ledger, accounts payable, and accounts receivable accounting modules;

- conducting regular training classes for all levels of users.

In my current position, I regularly work with department managers to assess their data processing needs and implement the correct solutions. As a Senior Systems Analyst, I offer direction to two COBOL programmers and our computer operator.

With my experience, I believe I can do an outstanding job for your company. Please contact me at my office (617-555-0250) or home (617-555-6346) to arrange a meeting. Thank you for your consideration.

Sincerely,

Jeffrey P. Chomansky
7 Bunker Hill Rd.
Newton, MA 02161

John R. O'Neal
234 Pratt Avenue
Gulfport, MS 39501
(601) 555-1892

September 1, 1994

Ms. Michelle Arnold
Eye World of Gulfport
400 W. Beach Blvd.
Gulfport, MS 39501

Dear Ms. Arnold:

When I read your advertisement for an office manager/controller, I was struck by how closely the requirements of the position align with my experience and skills. Please consider these qualifications in light of your stated needs:

I directly supervised a staff of seven professionals; I also indirectly supervised the departmental budgets and expenditures of more than thirty cost-center managers.

• I used my communications skills extensively to brief the executive staff.

• As Chief Financial Officer, I was directly responsible for all financial matters, and I was recognized quickly for my abilities.

• I have gained a broad knowledge of accounting from my academic and professional experiences.

• My computer skills are well developed from both managerial and individual-user perspectives.

• I was responsible for the first- and third-party reimbursement program, which was consistently rated among the best for collection percentages.

I will contact your office within a week regarding an interview. If, on reviewing my credentials in the meantime, you agree that I am the person you need, please contact me at (601) 555-1892.

Thank you for your time and consideration.

Cordially,

John R. O'Neal

Office Manager/Controller
For eyecare facility. Supervisory experience required. Successful candidate will take responsibility for company budget. Excellent communications and computer skills needed. Strong skills in finance and accounting a must. Knowledge of insurance reimbursement systems preferred. Write to:
Ms. Michelle Arnold
Eye World of Gulfport
400 W. Beach Blvd.
Gulfport, MS 39501

David Kopetman
85 W. 85th Street
New York, NY 10023
212-555-1960

January 23, 1994

Ms. Amy Grant
Manhattan Engineering Supplies
23 Houston Street
New York, NY 10005

Dear Ms. Grant,

In my four years as sales manager of a leading engineering supplies distributor in Long Island, I directed the sales and marketing policies of the company's line of drafting parts and accessories.

During that time:

- Annual billings more than tripled from $3.25 million to $10.75 million.

- Profits rose five-fold, from $150,000 in 1984 to $785,000 for the fiscal year ending September, 1988.

- Number of accounts within the same geographical territory increased by more than 250 percent.

The success I've had here and elsewhere in fifteen years of selling is not a coincidence, or attributable to luck or magic. My sales success is due to my education in Business Administration (Cornell, 1979) and a natural ability to analyze a marketing/selling situation and come up with an innovative program that leaves the competition way behind.

What I have done for my previous employers, I am confident I can do for you.

Ms. Grant, I will be calling you next week so that we can discuss how I can serve your company in increasing sales and market share. In the meantime, please feel free to contact me at 212-555-1960. Thank you for your time and consideration.

Sincerely yours,

David Kopetman

Dr. Anthony Kleiman
34 Handhewn Way
Manlius, NY 13104
(315) 555-2323
Kleiman@orange.
syracuse.edu

July 28, 1994

Chair of the Search Committee
Section of Plant Biology
State University of New York
Rochester, NY 14610

Dear Search Committee Chair:

The congruity of my scientific research, my teaching and program-management experience and your requirements would assure my success in the position of Professor and Chairperson of the Section of Plant Biology that you advertised on the bionet plants mail news group, July 28, 1994. In particular, the following characteristics and abilities may be of interest to you:

• Experience in supervising and motivating collaborators. During my appointment at Syracuse University, I was in charge of planning and conducting courses in plant physiology, anatomy, and evolution.

• A talent for organizing interdisciplinary teamwork. At the National Institutes of Health in Bethesda, MD, I had the pleasure of cooperating with experts in the areas of phytopathology, virology, immunology, mathematical modeling, image processing, and biomedical engineering. While at Syracuse University, I initiated collaborations with the departments of chemistry, biochemistry, mass spectrometry, and nuclear magnetic resonance.

• Extensive experience in scientific research. My latest work is concerned with macromolecular analysis and the development of innovative tools for the characterization of intact viruses, cell organelles, and large DNA molecules using nondenaturing techniques.

I offer an enthusiastic approach, a consistent work ethic, and diverse experience in all aspects of program management and interdisciplinary scientific research, as any of my colleagues can verify. One of my goals would be to provide academic and administrative leadership to promote excellence in teaching and research in the Section of Plant Physiology.

Thank you for your consideration. I look forward to the opportunity to explain in greater detail how I can be effective in this position. Should you have any questions, you may call me at (315) 555-2323.

Sincerely,

Anthony Kleiman, Ph.D.

Sarah Dent
3256 N. A1A, #34
Vero Beach, FL 32963
(407) 555-8118

February 22, 1993

Mr. Doug Jackson
Science Fiction Channel
200 Madison Avenue
New York, NY 10022

Dear Mr. Jackson:

You are about to enter a dimension as vast as space and as timeless as infinity. It is the middle ground between light and shadow, between science and superstition, and it lies between the pit of man's fears and the summit of his knowledge. This is the dimension of imagination. It is an area we call...The Sci-Fi Channel.

To bridge the gap between man's fears and the summit of his knowledge, you will need competent legal counsel who understands both the cable arena and science fiction. I am applying to be that counsel to The Sci-Fi Channel.

I can bring to this position not only quality legal counsel, but a passion for science fiction, extraordinary research experience, and even a broadcasting background that ranges from Jeopardy contestant to finalist in the network management division of the Academy of Television Arts and Sciences Program.

I will graduate from Stetson University College of Law in April and take the Florida Bar in July. My degree emphasizes corporate and media law. My legal work experience has focused on governmental law, and I am experienced in dealing with all varieties of bureaucrats.

Through my undergraduate major in communications, with an emphasis in film, media, public relations, and journalism, I have developed a keen understanding of cablecasting, as well as the ability to communicate effectively.

I'd like to telephone you before visiting your area in April to pinpoint a time when we could meet to discuss the excellent fit between my background and your needs. Thanks so much for your time and attention.

Best wishes,

Sarah Dent

April Greenberg
13 Winding Way
Atlanta, GA 30308

March 8, 1994

Mr. Sam Squash
VP, Public Relations
Georgia-Pacific, Inc.
Atlanta, GA 30308

Dear Mr. Squash,

In my last two editing positions, a thirty-gallon trash can in my office has been the destination of 90 percent of the press releases I received. I could write a book or teach a course on how not to write a news release or mount a publicity campaign.

I know what editors are looking for. I know because for the past year and a half, I was executive editor of a group of ten weekly newspapers in the Atlanta area. Before that, I was city editor for the newspaper in Georgia's third-largest city. I'm now managing editor of a new consumer magazine that, unfortunately, is relocating to California soon.

My inside track on the media would be enormously useful in running the public relations department. I have good contacts in the press and the knowledge of how to approach the media. I also have the ability to handle breaking news of the sort that presents great challenges to Fortune 500 companies such as Georgia Pacific.

Finally, I have considerable successful management experience, having supervised as many as thirty reporters and editors simultaneously. I also have the exceptional organizational skills needed to create media plans.

I'd like to set up an interview at your convenience and will call you at the beginning of the month to schedule it. You may also reach me during business hours at 404-555-2660 or leave a message at 404-555-9528. Thanking you most kindly for your consideration of me, I look forward to meeting with you soon.

Cordially,

April Greenberg

Mr. Jim R. Chapman
Human Resources
Christenson Engineering
Corporation
P.O. Box 5281
Bellingham, WA 98227-5281

February 14, 1993

Dear Mr. Chapman:

Dr. Burbank N. Rayos suggested that I write to you regarding the position of Senior Human Resources Assistant and its requirement for someone who can maintain a steady course despite many interruptions.

Let's talk about interruptions. Whoops, there's the phone. Excuse me.... Sorry about that, now where was I. Oh yes, I was explaining that interruptions aren't a problem. I can keep many complex projects going at once and haven't yet pulled out all my hair.

I'm assuming by "self-starter" you mean someone who finds out the criteria for the desired outcome and simply goes and does it, checking in whenever it's appropriate. That's how I like to work, and I've done it well according to my supervisors.

I am a grown-up. I like to take on responsibility. I learn very quickly, I have a good attitude, and I thrive on making my boss successful.

Now here's the thing. My experience is not actually in Personnel, but, here's what I can offer—a master's degree in organization development with a lot of related study in human resources such as employee enrichment, meeting-design and facilitation, training and development, and a little continuous quality improvement thrown in for good measure. I decided to switch careers, so I went back to graduate school, and Human Resources is where I want to be. I think you'll find that my experience, plus my general smarts and whole-systems approach will be valuable to your organization.

I look forward to the opportunity of meeting with you and will call you next week to make an appointment.

Sincerely,

Sheri Kelling
1251 H Street #4
Bellingham, WA 98225
days 206-555-9733

Jay Bayne
101 Church Street
Mobile, AL 36608
(205) 555-2124

Oct. 24, 1994

Dr. Amy Barrett
University of Central Florida
Department of Biology
Orlando, FL 32816

Dear Dr. Barrett:

You would not know that I am an avid fisherman from reading my resume. But then neither would you realize that I am adaptable, aggressively intellectual, cooperative, goal orientated, and a team player. I take great pleasure in the theories and practices of science and in the possibility of contributing to an ever-growing pool of knowledge.

I am applying for the Biologist Assistant position because I enjoy field biology and have a deep interest in conservation. My past experiences have involved extensive radiotelemetry work on a variety of species. I have independently tracked 30+ raccoons, studied radio-tagged Mexican spotted owls in southern Utah, and aided in the release of three tagged peregrine falcons. I am familiar with a variety of telemetry equipment, as well as the analysis of telemetry data.

Coupled with my extensive telemetry work is a thorough knowledge of orienteering, including the use of compasses and GPS's. My graduate work provided bountiful opportunities to practice and refine my technical writing skills, including the preparation of a thesis and biannual reports of my progress to the funding agency.

I am excited about the position, and I would appreciate the opportunity to work for you. My former employers can attest that if you hired me you would be getting a sincere, hardworking wildlife biologist.

I hope this letter introduces me well and that you take the opportunity to get to know me better through my resume. I would enjoy talking to you on the phone or visiting the area to learn more about UCF and the position, so I'll call you next week to see if we can pinpoint a time to meet.

Sincerely,

Jay Bayne

Judy Wood
4354 Winter Ave.
Los Angeles, CA 98765
(213) 555-8832

October 10, 1994

Mr. Kirk Horton
Human Resources Manager
Fantastic Software
P.O. Box 1234
Mountain View, CA 94045

Dear Mr. Horton:

Are you seeking an experienced product marketing professional? Could you use a marketer whose efforts contributed to a flagship product's 800 percent increase in sales revenues over three years? I am that marketer.

As the Director of Marketing at Pegboard Press Publishing, I enjoyed the opportunity to be involved in every aspect of marketing, from strategic planning to package design to managing successful product launches. My contributions to Pegboard resulted in its flagship product, *Hearth and Home Cookbook*, achieving and maintaining the top position in its category.

I am confident that my consumer software marketing experience, and my ability to successfully manage budgets, schedules, and project teams would enable me to contribute significantly to Fantastic Software. My outstanding analytical and communication skills, strong customer focus, creativity, and enthusiasm would be valuable assets as well.

Should an appropriate position become available, I would greatly appreciate the opportunity to discuss my qualifications with you. I'll phone you during the next quarter to check on openings. You may also reach me at (213) 555-8832. Thank you very much for your consideration and I look forward to meeting with you.

Sincerely,

Judy Wood

Gretchen Addams
1050 W. 100th Circle
Westminster, CO 80021
(303) 555-5683

September 18, 1994

Isabel Hughes, Program Director
WDYZ
100 Rocky Mountain Road
Denver, CO 80230

Dear Ms. Hughes,

Because I have developed and produced an informative celebrity-interview show and have done Air Talent shifts at several radio stations, I believe I have the qualities to serve in an Air Talent/Talk Show Host capacity at your station.

Talkfest, the show I oversaw from its inception to its current success, featured interviews with such celebrities as radio personality Don Imus, actors Tom Hanks and Cybill Shepherd, talk-show host Phil Donahue, U. S. Senator Ted Kennedy of Massachusetts, and many others. I've enclosed a tape of *Talkfest* highlights.

Former station managers can tell you that I'm organized, dependable, and able to handle multiple tasks. I'm not only a talented announcer, but am deft at production, able to write copy, news and sports, and can manage front-desk duties.

I believe it would be mutually fruitful for us to discuss how I can contribute to your station's ongoing success. I will contact you next week to set up a meeting. If you'd like to reach me before that, please call (303) 555-5683.

Thanks so much, Ms. Hughes, for considering me.

Sincerely,

Gretchen Addams

Sammy Pietro
29 Hillsdale Drive
Battle Creek, MI
(616) 555- 1336

September 13, 1994

Mr. Mariah Fisch
President
National Steel
Mishawaka, IN 46544

Dear Mr. Fisch,

During eighteen years of manufacturing experience, most of it in project management, I've made it a priority to continually develop my business skill set with an eye toward the future. Manufacturing Production Control has provided me with the opportunity to gain wide experience in manufacturing systems, demonstrate my ability to successfully lead projects, and develop the discipline required to perform while standing at the center of the storm.

I'd like to bring those skills to your company. I will fulfill my personal goal of ten years with Harris Semiconductor in October. I would be very interested in talking with you about opportunities at National Steel.

As Harris Semiconductor Military & Aerospace Division Project Leader charged with the implementation of our Integrated Manufacturing Production Requirements Scheduling System (IMPRESS), I reported directly to the Plant Manager and was responsible for weekly progress presentations to the VP/GM and his staff. The project touched every corner of our business and my implementation teams came from every major functional discipline. I'm proud to say that IMPRESS is now the backbone of our factory system integration.

I'd like to meet with you to see if I can do for you what I did for Harris. I'll contact you in two weeks to arrange a meeting.

Regards,

Sammy Pietro

283 E. Central Avenue
Moorestown, NJ 08507
609-555-5665

September 14, 1994

Mr. Stephen McMann
McMann & Stevens Advertising
100 University Blvd., 15th Floor
Princeton, NJ 08540

Dear Mr. McMann,

As advertising agencies are increasingly being evaluated on the development of advertising campaigns that guarantee success, there is a growing need for trained and experienced professionals in the field.

Through my advertising experience and my master's degree in marketing, I am certain I could give you valuable assistance in satisfying client demands for top-quality work, while also providing strong leadership skills.

I will be completing my master's degree in December and would be interested in making a contribution to McMann & Stevens Advertising's profitability in a client-services capacity.

I believe my experience and talents would be useful to you, and I will call you in late September to discuss an interview.

Thank you for your time and consideration. I look forward to speaking with you.

Sincerely,

Krystan V. Siesnen

232 Mountain Drive
Denver, CO 80210
303-555-2332

Ms. Samantha Montgomery
First Colorado Insurance Co.
75 Mountain Lakes Drive
Denver, CO 80210

Dear Ms. Montgomery,

According to the local newspaper, there were more than 200 "suspicious" fires in Denver in 1993. Of those 200+ fires, only about 20 were ever officially logged as arson. That's less than a 10 percent success ratio.

My 15 years as a fire marshall with the Denver Fire Department and my seven years as fire investigator with Rocky Mountain Insurance Company, Inc.—where my arson success ratio is close to 50 percent, should qualify me for the position of Chief Fire Investigator.

My work with the arson squad of the Denver Fire Department earned high praise and three citations from the mayor's office. My work with Rocky Mountain has saved the company millions of dollars in fraudulent fire claims.

Although I am happy in my present job and Rocky Mountain is certainly more than satisfied with my work, I feel it's time to move from being a player to becoming a manager, where, with my keen sense of investigating, I can lead a team and help your company save millions of dollars.

I would like to discuss my qualifications more fully with you in the near future. I will call you next Tuesday to see if we can find an agreeable time.

Thank you for your time and consideration.

Sincerely,

Daniel Swanson

Michael D. Reynolds
PO Box 231
Tellico Plains, TN 37385
615-555-2358
mdreynol@aol.com

October 8, 1994

Mr. Judson Beasley
VP, Marketing & Distribution
Coca-Cola, Inc.
Atlanta, GA 30313

Dear Mr. Beasley,

I am a seasoned professional and highly successful and competent team member with a background of extensive "hands on" experience in manufacturing, service, and distribution market segments. My success has been both inward to the operating unit level and outward to the financial and supplier entities. I'd like to bring that success to your company in a marketing distribution capacity.

As a profit-oriented manager with a proven track record and a bias toward responsible growth and effective utilization of costs and overhead, I bring an absolutely positive "can do!" attitude to the work place. "But we have never done it that way" is NOT an operational part of my vocabulary.

I am well versed in the applicable concepts and implementation of managerial and fiscal reporting necessary for a successful business enterprise. I have experience with various text and word processing applications; computer languages such as Clarion, BASIC and INFORMIX and various report writers; applications such as MAPICS, SOTAS, ACCPAC, and BAS as well as industry-specific packages. I have been extremely successful in accounting system conversions between heterogeneous systems.

Relocation is not an impediment. I am willing to travel extensively.

I believe it would be worthwhile for us to meet. I will contact you in a week to arrange a meeting. Should you have any questions before that time, please feel free to reach me by phone at 615-555-2358, or by email at mdreynol@aol.com.

Very truly yours,

Michael D. Reynolds

103 Andrew Jackson Street,
Apt 32
Milwaukee, Wisconsin
53202
Tel: (414) 555-3471
Fax: (414) 555-1003

October 15, 1994

Ms. Carol Seachrist
Mascotech, Inc.
Taylor, MI 48180

Dear Ms. Seachrist:

My solid experience in project leadership, full life-cycle development of sales-force automation systems, trouble-shooting, and customer support, combined with my background in client-server and relational databases, would enable me to enhance your success in software development at Mascotech, Inc. Both my master's and bachelor's degrees are in computer science with a minor in accounting.

As any of my former employers can attest, I am a self motivated, hands-on, results-oriented person who continuously demonstrates a high level of commitment and a strong work ethic. I am also a strong team player who will exert every effort to ensure that the goals of the team are met.

Thanks to my technical background, as well as my clear understanding of the customer's business process, I am recognized as a valuable resource for providing input and ideas. My excellent communication skills and accurate verbal content allow me to effectively communicate with people at all levels.

This combination of skills gives me a solid foundation upon which to make an immediate and meaningful contribution to your establishment. If upon reviewing my qualifications you agree that I would be able to contribute to the plans and goals of Mascotech, I would be pleased to meet with you to further discuss my background. I will contact you the week of October 24th to arrange a meeting. Should you have any questions before that time, you may reach me at (414) 555-3471 or by email at Pesmen@highlife.wisconson.edu.

Thank you for your time and consideration.

Sincerely,

Ross Pesmen

Stanley Lucas
262 Buckhead Lane
Atlanta, GA 30026
(404) 555-3292

February 2, 1994

Mr. Dabney Greer
Director of Marketing
National Service Industries, Inc.
Atlanta, GA 30310

Dear Mr. Greer:

As you know, it's the hottest companies that need extra resources during crunch times, so you might want to keep my card close at hand.

I recently relocated to Atlanta from San Francisco, where I worked as the Information Designer in Macromedia, Inc.'s creative-services department. There, I wrote the company's marketing collateral—from product data sheets, packaging and position papers to video-scripts.

I have a strong background in marketing and public relations, great product-management skills, and a working knowledge of the most popular graphics and multimedia-authoring software.

My broad range of skills makes it easy for me to jump in and get the job done. Whether you need new marketing collateral for your company or a new product, a story pitched to the media, assistance in planning for an upcoming trade show, or extra help in finishing a multimedia production—my skills may be just what you need.

So do keep me in mind during your next crunch period. I'd be happy to send you samples of my work and talk with you about how my skills and experience could be strong assets for National Service Industries, Inc. I'll call you to touch base after the Multimedia convention; maybe I'll even see you there.

Sincerely,

Stanley Lucas

Lisa Anne Knauth
3238 NE 34th Avenue
Cape Coral, FL 33904
(813) 555-4322

April 3, 1993

Mr. James Griffin
Atlanta Olympic Organizing Committee
500 Peachtree Street
Atlanta, GA 30308

Dear Mr. Griffin:

As you and the Atlanta Olympic Organizing Committee bring an international event to the South, you will be seeking people with good organizational and networking skills. I am one of those people. In response to your advertisement in the Orlando Sentinel, I am interested in augmenting the committee's operation in a legal or management capacity.

My legal work experience has been mainly in government and environmental law, while my academic background has been primarily in international law and communications, with an emphasis on broadcasting and public relations.

During a diverse career as an archivist, law clerk, and workshop instructor, I have developed organizational and networking skills, a talent for efficiently gathering information from government officials and written sources, and the ability to work well with clients on various projects.

The committee will be required to coordinate with various organizations, media outlets, federations, and corporations to present these Games in style, objectives that will require staff that can travel well, communicate effectively, and work independently. I have traveled in the United States and overseas, speak and write fluent French, and have written about television for two publications. I am also the problem-solver around the law school—the one students consult when they need help untangling the bureaucracy.

I will contact you at the end of the month to arrange a convenient interview time. Should you wish to contact me, please do so at my Cape Coral address. Thank you for your consideration.

Sincerely,

Lisa Anne Knauth

372 Main Street
Los Altos, CA 94022
(310) 555-3334

October 15, 1994

Ms. JoAnn Greenfield
Planned Parenthood, Inc.
P.O. Box 383
Mountain View, CA 94045

Dear Ms. Greenfield:

My degree in nutrition and my work with the Women, Infants, and Children supplemental food program align nicely with your needs in the research-assistant position you are currently advertising.

My work with the American Heart Association, which focused on the prevention of coronary heart disease through a healthy lifestyle, would be extremely helpful in developing a clearinghouse of wellness/health promotion.

I could also bring legislative-staff and task-force experience to the wellness/health program as I have a thorough understanding of the operations of California government.

Ms. Greenfield, I believe my qualifications are an excellent fit with this position and that it would be expedient for us to meet. I will give you a call early next week to set up an interview.

Thank you for your consideration.

Sincerely,

Kimberly Long

Phil Caldwell
327 Handy Way
Normal, IL 61761
(815) 555-2234

May 30, 1994

Dr. Mavis Fennelly
Department of Engineering
Illinois State University
Normal, IL 61760

Dear Dr. Fennelly,

Would you like your Engineering Center Manager to be someone who has conducted extensive research on the major obstacles to successful careers in engineering? Someone who has a solid applied background as an award-winning, mechanical engineer? Someone with the experience and pedagogical ideas needed to teach engineering skills effectively? Someone with advanced proficiency with computers and CAD? I have the experience and vision that would enable me to make a real difference to the Engineering Center.

I am currently researching and developing a career guide for college engineering students. One aspect of this research has been to survey college faculty members nationwide on the major problems that they encounter with engineering students. As a result of this research, I have a solid understanding of the major problem areas, and I have developed techniques for targeting the barriers to successful careers in engineering.

I am completely adept on the Macintosh. In addition to using Macintosh systems in my job for the last several years, I've had my own Mac system at home for more than seven years. My knowledge of PCs includes a thorough understanding of the DOS and Windows environments, and my abilities to use PCs is superior.

I have enclosed a supplemental sheet outlining my engineering accomplishments, one of the highlights of which is my three and a half year tenure as director of the engineering department at a subsidiary of United Technologies.

I have tutored dozens of students in engineering skills and have developed syllabi for engineering courses. I am thoroughly committed to helping college students develop engineering skills to become successful not only as students, but in their careers—and in life.

Dr. Fennelly, I am eager to meet with you. I'll call you at the beginning of next week to arrange a mutually convenient time. Should you wish to reach me, you may call me at home at (815) 555-2234 or at work at (815) 555-5500.

Thanks so much for your interest and attention.

Cordially,

Phil Caldwell

328 W. Joyce Kilmer Court
Salt Lake City, UT 84106
(801) 555-4343

March 16, 1994

Mr. Sam James
Movies Unlimited
100 Main Street
Salt Lake City, UT 84105

Dear Mr. James,

Congratulations on the opening of your new store. Your ad leads me to believe you and I share a philosophy about customer service. That's why I'm eager to bring my experience in working with the public, combined with a love of movies and a near-photographic memory that enables me to quickly learn stock, to the customer-service representative position you are advertising for the new eastside Movies Unlimited store.

Although you will note from the enclosed application and resume that my retail experience is not very recent, I have a steady and reliable work history of positions that would make me an excellent worker for your store.

I am a mature college student at BYU. I have just a very few credit-hours to finish up this summer and fall to obtain my degree, and I could easily work those few classes around a full and flexible schedule at Movies Unlimited. I am perfectly willing to work evenings, weekends, and holidays.

I truly believe Movies Unlimited and I are an excellent fit. What's really important to me is to contribute to your bottom line while working with interesting people and movies— close to home.

I'm intelligent, and any of my references and previous employers can tell you that I am a hard worker. Mr. James, I hope you'll give me a chance to show you how I can enhance your new operation. Shall we meet soon so you can learn more about my skills? I'll call you next week to make an appointment.

Thanks very much.

Cordially,

Cynthia Davis

Robert Z. Flint
1861 E. 39th Street
Brooklyn, NY 11229
(718) 555-3264

July 3, 1994

Mr. Sean Jackson
NBC-TV
Rockefeller Center
New York, NY 10020

Dear Mr. Jackson:

A work history can tell you only the bare bones of my story. You can get that from the enclosed resume. This letter is to help you get to know me.

I am a broadcaster, experienced in the radio and television fields. Though I've worked for several radio and television affiliates in my career, this is the field in which I've determined I can make the biggest difference. I'd like to make that difference in the producer job you are advertising.

Hands on! That's how I learned and how I work. My goal is to become indispensable to a station. When given the opportunity to bring my enthusiasm to your workplace, I can show you the difference between being just an employee and being a driven, goal-oriented team player. That is exactly what I did in my last job at the NBC affiliate in Albany.

Within a few days of your receiving this letter, I'll call on you personally to arrange a face-to-face meeting. I am looking forward to working with you, learning your style, and bringing some of mine to the network as well.

Sincerely,

Robert Z. Flint

Sarah Rose Burbank
3283 Longhorn Drive
Austin, TX 78712
(512) 555-2821

May 8, 1991

Mr. James Jenkins, Training Manager
Department of Human Resources
Blue Cross/Blue Shield of New Mexico
12800 Indian School Rd.
Albuquerque, NM 87112

Dear Mr. Jenkins,

My experience as a teacher and writer qualifies me to fill the position you advertised in the May 5, 1994 edition of the Albuquerque Journal for independent contractors to teach business English.

I have had extensive experience teaching writing at various levels, from Remedial Writing to Advanced Expository Prose and Creative Writing–Prose Fiction, at the University of New Mexico and the University of Albuquerque; additionally, I have taught traditional grammar.

As a university instructor and as an instructor for the University of Texas, I have taught adults exclusively. I have received excellent evaluations from my students, especially those in Advanced Expository Prose, and have been asked by students to offer independent studies courses in writing and research when my regular sections were filled to capacity.

As a professional technical writer, both as an independent contractor and with a local firm, Strategic Communication, Inc., I am qualified to teach technical writing.

I think you'll agree that a meeting would be both appropriate and mutually beneficial. Please allow me to call you within the next few weeks to arrange an appointment.

Thank you very much for your consideration.

Sincerely,

Sarah Rose Burbank

Linda Smith
2053 Dogwood Lane
Tallahassee, FL 32303
904-555-9219

August 23, 1994

Dear Boxholder,

Certain key words in your ad lead me to believe I may well be the perfect candidate for this retail opening, and I'm ready to make a real contribution.

Organizing is a magic word to me because it's what I do best. Virtually all my previous positions have required a detail-oriented and successful organizer to pull everything together. Nowhere has this been more true than in my current position as a production manager in New York's largest ad agency.

Retail environment evokes satisfying memories of the work I did in my last position as men's apparel buyer for Burdines. I thrive in the fast pace and exciting atmosphere of retailing, as the enclosed letter of recommendation from Dawn Bachman will attest to.

Advertising and publicity are magic words because I have lots to contribute in these two areas. My previous positions have always given me a certain involvement in promotional strategy, especially as sales manager for Beaumont Leather Goods, Inc. Combined with my academic experience in advertising and marketing, I have a well-rounded portfolio of services to add to your sales and profits.

Career opportunity is perhaps the most magic phrase of all as I have long been searching for a job that I could fully develop long-term. This one seems so perfect because it combines my interest and experience in retail with my organizational talents and promotions expertise.

I would be most happy to make myself available for an interview at your convenience.

Thank you for your consideration, I look forward to hearing from you in the very near future.

Sincerely,

Linda Smith

302 Bentley Circle
Champaign, IL 61820
312-555-5342

April 10, 1994

Mr. Scott Lucas
Quaker Oats, Inc.
Chicago, IL 60606

Dear Mr. Lucas,

Because I've recently completed a major overhaul of Star Cookies at General Foods Corp., your display ad in last Sunday's Tribune for a Brand Manager at Quaker Oats is of special interest to me since it calls for qualifications that completely correspond to my background.

As you can see on my resume, in addition to an excellent professional background in brand management, I have had particular success with new product introductions, twice being promoted because of my ideas and innovations.

While my successes have come often, I feel I have gone as far as I can with General Foods, and am ready to take on new challenges at Quaker Oats. I have had ten solid years of brand management experience and now want to bring my ideas and knowledge to your firm.

May I ask you to read my resume and then allow me to phone your secretary next week for an appointment? In the interim, please feel free to call me at 312-555-5342. I look forward to meeting you and thank you for your time and consideration.

Sincerely,

Thomas Burlington

101 Franklin Blvd.
Summit, NJ 07901
201-555-1010

August 2, 1994

Ms. Juliet Romanio
Al Borland Elementary School
4567 Springfield Avenue
Newark, NJ 07103

Dear Ms. Romanio,

Perhaps I am the "multi-talented teacher" you seek in your "Multi-Talented Teacher" advertisement in today's Newark Star-Ledger. I'm a versatile teacher, ready to substitute, if necessary, as early as next week. I have the solid teaching experience you specify.

As you will note on the enclosed resume, I am presently affiliated with a highly regarded private elementary school. Mr. Russell, the headmaster, will certainly give you a good reference.

The details of your advertisement suggest to me that the position will involve many of the same responsibilities that I am currently performing.

In addition to the planning, administrating, and student-parent counseling duties I highlight in my resume, please note that I have a master's degree as well as a teaching certificate from the state of New Jersey.

Knowing how frantic you must be without a fifth grade teacher, I will call you in a few days. Or if you agree upon reviewing my letter and resume that I am the teacher you need, call me at the home number listed above or at 555-1100 during business hours.

Thanking you most sincerely for your time and consideration.

Cordially,

Abigail Doyle

Patty Hathaway
17 Elm Court
Stamford, CT
(203) 555-1732

January 7, 1994

Mr. Edward Dascher
Personnel Director
Xerox Corp.
Stamford, CT 06902

Dear Mr. Dascher,

Your advertisement in today's Wall Street Journal stimulated my interest and seems to match exactly my particular background and skills.

You Require:	*My Qualifications:*
Advanced Degree	I have an MBA from the Wharton School, specializing in accounting
10 years accounting experience	4 years, Accountant at Philip Morris in large corporate environment; 3 years, Senior Accountant at AT&T; 4 years, Accounts, Price Waterhouse
Manager of EDP applications	Designed integrated EDP invoicing system for AT&T. IBM, Digital, mainframe experience.

Since my experience and knowledge fit your requirements exactly, I am clearly one of the people you'll want to see. I plan on calling you the week of January 14 to see about setting up an interview. In the meantime, please feel free to call me at my home number as listed above. I look forward to our meeting.

Thank you for your time and consideration.

Sincerely,

Patty Hathaway

Chad Lee Forte
480 Cotton Bay Drive, #44
West Palm Beach, FL 33406
(407) 555-1134

March 29, 1994

Mr. Marc Miller
Miller, Cohen & Company
1300 S. Olive Avenue
West Palm Beach, FL 33406

Dear Mr Miller,

I was very pleased to see your advertisement for an accountant that recently appeared in the Miami Herald because the position is well suited to both my professional and educational background.

The direct responsibilities of my position in the United States Navy closely parallel the requirements of your advertised position. It was solely my responsibility to manage, track, and report the financial position of the hospital, which included accounting for income statement and balance-sheet items. I also gained valuable experience in preparing short- (quarterly) to intermediate-length (annual) term budgets for the medical facility, which consisted of more than thirty specialized departments. To streamline the patchwork process, I employed my expertise at designing spreadsheets in Lotus 1-2-3, which were easily updated using various forecasting methods; this process enabled me to keep the hospital's dynamic financial outlook in clear focus.

In addition to my experience in the Navy, I have enjoyed numerous other accounting positions outside of the health-care field; I have another seven years' experience in both the restaurant and retail industries, during which I performed general-ledger accounting bank reconciliations, financial statement preparation, and most other accounting functions.

My educational background, while based in finance and business administration, has provided me with an in-depth knowledge of financial and managerial accounting practices. My long-term educational goals include the completion of the additional coursework necessary to obtain a Master of Accountancy degree and CPA certification.

My wife and I have recently moved to West Palm Beach, where she has begun a tenure-track faculty position in the School of Business Administration at Florida Atlantic University. Mr Miller, knowing how pressed you must be to fill this position, I will contact your office within a week regarding an interview. If, on reviewing my credentials in the meantime, you agree that I am the person you need, please contact me at the home number listed above.

Cordially,

Chad Lee Forte

Kenneth Vasonova
393 Peach Tree Drive, #7
Naperville, IL 60042.
618-555-2390

September 19, 1994

S. A. Ying
Becton Dickinson & Co.
Des Plaines, IL 60016

Dear S. A. Ying,

The ad for a mechanical engineer position in the Sept. 10 National Ad Search leads me to believe you seek a person with my ability to handle multiple tasks while meeting high efficiency standards and reducing costs.

With both a bachelor's and master's degree in mechanical engineering, I am well qualified for the position described. I have a strong technical background in design and analysis. In my position as a materials engineer for a medical-electronics company, I am accustomed to working in a fast-paced environment.

I seek a challenging position that provides the opportunity to work hard to help the company attain its goals.

I look forward to talking with you so that I can share with you my background and enthusiasm for the job. I will contact you in ten days to arrange a meeting. Should you wish to reach me in the meantime, please feel free to call me at (618) 555-2390. If I am not in, please leave a message and I will return your call within a day.

Thank you for your time and consideration.

Sincerely,

Kenneth Vasonova

Monique Anne Bleuel
128 Watergate Blvd., #12
Washington, D.C. 20015
(202) 555-1224

October 2, 1994

Box 435
Washington Post
Washington, D.C. 20009

Dear Boxholder:

My work as both the Chief Financial Officer and Chief of Computer Systems Management at the Washington Qwik-Care provides me with a solid background to contribute to the success of your firm in the COO/Medical Data Processing position advertised in the Post.

As Chief Financial Officer, I was responsible for all first- and third-party billings for medical services rendered. In times of rising health care costs, my department made aggressive efforts to collect funds due to the center; successful collections could then be incorporated into the operating budget.

As Chief of Computer Systems Management, I was responsible for every aspect of computer operations within the center—from large projects, such as bringing entirely new networks on-line to smaller tasks, such as performing system backups.

I will contact your office within a week regarding an interview. If, on reviewing my credentials in the meantime, you agree that I am the person you need, please contact me at the home number listed above.

Cordially,

Monique Anne Bleuel

54 Blue Crab Drive, #278
Columbia, MD 21044
301-555-5233

October 10, 1994

Director of Human Resources
Box T621
Times, NY 10018

Dear Director of Human Resources,

My knack for numbers coupled with more than five years of accounting experience make me an ideal candidate for the accounting supervisor position you advertised for in the Sunday New York Times.

In my present position with Carnegie Mellon Accounting, Inc., I further developed my management skills as well as a strong knowledge of financial accounting. Through the use of this knowledge and experience, I was able to greatly improve the manner in which financial accounting was conducted.

By devising and applying new systems that utilized personnel and equipment more efficiently, I significantly reduced operating costs and time spent recording routine financial transactions. The end result was a more efficient organization offering higher quality financial accounting services.

I strongly feel that my experience and enthusiasm for doing quality financial accounting would be a good addition to your organization. I look forward to your response and the opportunity to further discuss the possibility of working for your company. I'll call you five days hence to schedule a meeting; feel free also to call me at the telephone number listed above.

Thank you for your time and consideration.

Sincerely,

Venessa Camden White

Fred N. Allegro
23 Library Lane
Plainview, NY 11803
(516) 555-2921

October 14, 1994

UU245
Times 10108

Dear Boxholder:

As I read your ad in the New York Times for a research manager, I knew immediately that I could offer exactly the solid marketing-research experience and analytical skills you describe.

In my current position as a marketing analyst for a market-research firm, I have projected future growth of various industries by researching and analyzing past performance. My analytical skills have contributed to my ability to solve and prevent problems both in my current position and in a previous position with a list broker.

I could bring to your marketing-research position the finely honed communications skills that would enable me to translate research data into readable language. I currently write press releases and direct-mail marketing brochures.

My college thesis, "Developing Cost-Effective Advertising Campaigns," demonstrates my thorough understanding of magazine advertising and other media that compete for advertising dollars.

I also possess considerable supervisory skills, having successfully motivated subordinates and coordinated their activities.

I believe my qualifications and your needs are an excellent fit. I think it would be in both our best interests to meet. I can make myself available for an appointment at your earliest convenience. Please feel free to call me at (516) 555-2921.

Sincerely,

Fred N. Allegro

Tiffany Sipowitz
400 Carter Street
Chattanooga, TN 37402
(615) 555-0218

December 10, 1994

Managing Partner
P.O. Box 5555
Chattanooga, TN 37410-5555

Dear Managing Partner:

I note that your needs for the Executive Secretary/Administrative Assistant position you are currently advertising coincide with my skills and experience. The ad particularly details the core requirements of my position at Cravens, Smythe, and Harrison, P.A., a management function at which I enjoyed great success.

The environment of the law firm at which I worked was composed of diverse professionals. What I found to be most productive for the operation was developing cooperative working relationships with the staff. In this setting, a judicious mixture of solid interpersonal skills, adaptability to others' needs, and a sincere demeanor was needed. I worked hard to emphasize these traits to my staff, and we built an efficient and cohesive team that was recognized as highly competent and customer-service oriented.

My department administered the financial/accounting and information-system needs for the entire facility. The law firm utilized information-system networks for various functions, including accounts payable, billings, and productivity accounting. I have also gained in-depth knowledge of these and other accounting functions from my undergraduate and graduate studies. The office automation LAN used Wordperfect 5.1 and Lotus 1-2-3.

Although I have an MBA, I plan to add further accounting coursework to my education and eventually sit for the CPA exam.

Should you wish to reach me for an interview, you may call or leave a message at (615) 555-0218. Although I will be out of the area from the 16th through the 31st to spend the holidays with my family, I plan to review my phone messages frequently. In addition, I will be available for work immediately after my return. I look forward to talking with you.

Sincerely,

Tiffany Sipowitz

Gonzalo Lopez
87454 Plymouth Avenue
Alexander City, AL 35010
(205) 555-2912
E-Mail: Gonzo@AOL.COM

April 23, 1994

TO: JOB-HJ50@COMMUNIX.COM

REF: Project Manager Position
   My extensive experience in project management and my commitment to assembling personnel-support teams that will get the job done align extremely well with the requirements of the above job that was posted on the Internet.
   I am very much oriented to managing projects/schedules, and my team-building experience would be an asset to any organization looking to get the most out of its human resources while controlling costs.
   I am also well versed in several software programs (Excel 5.0, Word Perfect and Microsoft Access) and the Windows environment. I have set up and operated a LAN and BBS system for management of U.S. government technical representatives over a wide geographical area and served on my agency's automatic data-processing selection/resourcing committee.
   I would like to be considered for a position in which someone of my background could make a contribution. I will contact you in ten days to arrange for a telephone or personal interview. Should you require any additional information, I can be contacted at the phone number listed above, by fax at (205) 555-7740 or by e-mail.

Very truly yours,

Gonzalo Lopez

Matt Coombes
123 Jones St.
Westport, CT 04321

203-555-1141
Coombes@highnet.com

February 20, 1994

Ms. Kelly Pickens
Director of Programming
Xerox, Inc.
Stamford, CT 06902
Kpickens@XPress.com

Dear Ms. Pickens,

I learned through the comp.databases.informix newsgroup that your corporation is seeking an Informix programmer. My strong commitment to a career in systems analysis and maintenance coupled with my programming experience make me a strong candidate for this position.

My experience in programming has enabled me to develop technical skills and allowed me to put computer training and theory into practical application.

I know Xerox has an extraordinary commitment to quality, and I would like to contribute to that commitment.

My previous supervisors will affirm that I am efficient, hardworking, and persistent.

If possible, a telephone interview with you to discuss my qualifications would be greatly appreciated. May I call you during the week of March 5th? Please feel free to contact me earlier at 203-555-1141 if you are so inclined.

Thank you for your time and consideration.

Sincerely,

Matt Coombes

Mr. Harry Fay
Ariel Computing
25340 Davies Ave.
Toronto, Ontario
M4K 1H3

October 5 1994

re: Intermediate PC Technician

Dear Mr. Fay,

Having worked on computers for ten years and having acquired a strong knowledge of many applications from word processors to drafting programs, I am prepared for success in the intermediate PC technician position you posted on tor.jobs.

I am familiar with several communications programs including Telix, Qmodem, and Procomm as well as SL/IP connection navigational tools.

My knowledge of hardware and technical procedures is a result of constant reconfiguration of my own home system as well as several years experience of development and maintenance of hospital and educational computer services. I have also acquired some formal training at the University of Toronto.

I have strong interpersonal and communication skills and enjoy working with all levels of computer users. In my job as coordinator of the Patient Computer Service at Toronto Teachers Hospital I took the opportunity to develop and maintain administrative procedures in accordance with the exacting standards of the Hospital Review Board.

Believing that my skills and experience are in the range of your requirements, I would welcome a chance to meet with you in person to discuss your need and my suitability in greater detail. I will contact you in a week to arrange a meeting. Should you have any questions before that time, please feel free to contact me at (416) 555-6504.

Thank you for considering me.

Sincerely,

Nancy Righter
283 Snowshoe Rd.
Toronto, Ontario M4L 2T8
voice: (416) 555-6504 • fax: (416) 555-6005
E-mail: Nancy@netcom.com

Lisa Short
3428 Ben Franklin Drive
Clemson, SC 29631
803-555-3483

June 20, 1994

Ms. Jane Wilson
General Electric Corp.
Fairfield, CT 06432

Dear Ms. Wilson:

Thank you for your interest in my resume. From what Roy Taylor told me about your company, an international research position sounds like a fascinating opportunity for me to contribute the knowledge I've learned on the Internet.

My resume details the skills I have acquired while working at Clemson University on various projects, such as setting up a Local Area Network for my cluster of dormitories. I'd like to focus your attention not only on my computer skills, but also on my ability to coordinate projects and work with others. My Spanish and Portuguese language skills and experience would enable me to make a significant contribution to your company when an international research position becomes available.

A recent assignment assisting the World Trade Center on an Asian Trade Mission project gave me international trade experience by providing the opportunity for me to contact various organizations in Tijuana, Mexicali, and Ensenada! Next month I plan to expand my global horizons by volunteering with "Grupo Esperanza" and will be building houses for a weekend in the outskirts of Tijuana.

Ms. Wilson, I will be checking up with you about once a month to see if your company may need my assistance. In the meantime, I will send you my resume in my next e-mail message. I would also like to request an informational interview, either in person or by phone, in which I could learn more about your company and how I might fit in.

Thank you for your time and consideration.

Best regards,

Lisa Short

Johnny Ritenougher
372 Speigel Drive
Chicago, IL 60600
(312) 555-2938

Mr. Steven Rhoads
Human Resources Director
Motorola, Inc.
Schaumberg, IL 60196

December 29, 1992

Dear Mr. Rhoads,

    I'd like to thank you for taking the time to discuss the recruitment officer position at Motorola with me. I very much appreciate the detail with which you described the position.

    I felt a rapport with you that I believe would contribute to an excellent working relationship.

    You did an exceptional job of emphasizing the importance of the position to the continuing success of the company. I am convinced that I can meet the challenge of exceeding federal and state government quotas for hirings.

    I also believe my experience in having worked well with students in my internship program and having made positive contacts with business people in my last several jobs would contribute significantly to the position. I could apply my considerable communications skills to giving presentations to graduating college seniors, and selling them on working at Motorola.

    I look forward to the possibility of a second interview and, even more, to the possibility of contributing to both the recruitment goals and the bottom line at Motorola. As I mentioned, I am immediately available for employment.

    Mr. Rhoads, thanks again for taking the time to meet with me.

Cordially,

Johnny Ritenougher

Debbie Papadeas
343 Tobacco Drive
Winston-Salem, NC 27105
(919) 555-2132

October 11, 1994

Dr. George Lennox
University of West Carolina
Winston-Salem, NC 27105

Dear Dr. Lennox:

I want to thank you for seeking me out and taking the time to meet with me about your proposed position of Special Assistant to the Provost for Admissions Projects. I am truly excited about this position and the contribution I could make toward working with alumni, high-school teachers, volunteers, faculty, and deans on recruitment, and targeting such potential student populations as nontraditional students, international students, and perhaps others.

My strong support for the University of Western Carolina, along with exceptional communications, organizational, promotional, and marketing skills, make me exactly the kind of "value-added" employee who can get this job done for you. You need someone who can target new kinds of student constituencies with innovative marketing skills. I believe I am that person.

My ability to "sell" Western Carolina has many dimensions, as the College of Medicine recently learned when Dean Deepknecht contracted with me to rewrite, edit, and polish both the overall School of Medicine accreditation plan and the Nursing Department plan. As you probably know, both documents earned the highest possible ratings from the accrediting bodies, and the college plans to contract with me for the next step in the accreditation documentation process.

My verbal ability to promote Western Carolina was demonstrated with the well-received commencement speech I gave at the fall 1993 commencement. To refresh your memory, I am enclosing a copy of that speech.

My work here at Western Carolina for the past year also speaks well of my ability to promote the university. I currently handle publicity and promotion for the Bolding Museum of Art. I also oversee the administration of the art department. I interact regularly with art majors, potential students, and the ten work-study students I supervise. My supervisors can unhesitatingly cite my superlative communications and organizational skills, as well as my high energy level. I have built on my past special-events-planning experience by producing regular museum receptions, and other events. As a current Western Carolina employee, I already have the advantage of having established working relationships with many members of the university community, as well as various external constituencies.

In our meeting, you cited the importance of the ability to handle important members of Western Carolina's constituencies with diplomacy. Having dealt successfully with a public-health advocacy network of some 500 people, with important statewide officials and politicians, and with donors and board members of Western Carolina's Friends of Art, I am confident of my ability to interact with the university's supporters who have good ideas.

I recently developed a new way to reach out to art-department alumni—a newsletter that accompanied a fund-raising mailing to this audience. I have enclosed a copy of this newsletter.

I demonstrated my ability to work directly with students, as well as my commitment to cultural diversity by creating a highly successful internship program for students at the University of Richmond and Virginia Tech. I focused on establishing hands-on, professional experiences for students in the communications office and elsewhere throughout the Virginia Department of Education. The internships were highly rated by student interns and sought after by their professors. The percentage of minority students I succeeded in recruiting to the program far exceeded the percentage of minority students in the student body at the University of Richmond.

As for number-crunching and spreadsheets, I would ask you to give me the chance to show you how quickly I can learn these skills. I won't let you down.

Finally, Dr. Lennox, I'm enclosing some ideas I've had for promoting Western Carolina and boosting enrollment. I note well your cautions that "everyone thinks they're an admissions expert." I don't pretend to be one, but I do want you to know that my mind is working on the challenges at hand.

Thank you again for your consideration of me. I look forward to the possibility of working with you.

Sincerely,

Debbie Papadeas

Craig Adelson
101 Fairmount Avenue
East Greenwich, RI 02818
(401) 555-9695

December 21, 1994

Dr. Peter Neuman
Greenwich Chiropractors, Inc.
200 E. Main Street
East Greenwich, RI 02818

Dear Dr. Neuman:

It was wonderful having the opportunity to speak with you concerning the nursing position with your practice. I know how limited a physician's time can be, and your timely involvement in the interview process impressed me. After speaking with you, I felt certain that we can develop an effective working relationship.

After reflecting on our discussion, I deduced that you are looking for more than a competent head nurse; you seek, perhaps, someone who can keep the entire operation in focus. Technical nursing skills are critical, and I can polish and execute mine readily. I intend to use not only my integrity and loyalty in this position, but my open communication and managerial skills to their fullest extent.

The scope of responsibility for this position is broad and parallels my position in the United States Army. I worked many additional hours to become proficient in the numerous areas of responsibility assigned to me, and my dedication and tenacity were quickly recognized. I would like to share the same experience with you in helping to contribute to the success of your organization.

If you decide that I should interview with any of your partners, I will be available at your convenience. Until then, I look forward to the possibility of working with you.

Sincerely yours,

Craig Adelson

Monique Anne Bleuel
128 Watergate Blvd., #12
Washington, D.C. 20010
(202) 555-1224

November 13, 1994

Dr. Jane Billings
Washington Hope Hospital
100 C Street NW
Washington, D.C. 20009

Dear Dr. Billings,

I'd like to thank you for talking with me about the COO position within your hospital. I also wish to take this opportunity to reiterate my interest in working for you at Washington Hope. I appreciate your comments concerning my qualifications and experience, and I feel very comfortable with the prospect of working with you.

After further studying the job description, I conclude that the ideal candidate should possess solid organizational and interpersonal skills, acute attention to detail, and a willingness to manage in a hands-on manner. The person selected for this position will also have to be a quick study to manage in a completely new environment and to ensure a smooth transition. I am convinced that I am a person whose skills and abilities align well with your needs.

This position is extremely similar to my position with Washington Qwik-Care, where I became proficient in management of the entire operation. In addition, my academic record attests to my dedication and penchant for learning.

If you decide that I should interview with the MIS Vice President and the Controller for Washington Hope, I will be available at your convenience.

Again, Dr. Billings, thank you for your time and consideration.

Cordially,

Monique Anne Bleuel

Karen Handelson
2780 Ben Franklin Drive,
#29
Philadelphia, PA
(215) 555-7495

October 27, 1994

Mr. John Easterbrook
Vice President of Accounting
Campbell Soup, Inc.
Camden, NJ 08101

Dear Mr. Easterbrook:

Thank you for taking the time to discuss the accounting assistant position with me. After meeting with you and observing the accounting operations, I am further convinced that my background and future goals coincide very well with your needs. I felt quite comfortable talking with you and Mr. Ralph Smith, and I am confident that we can work well together.

I really appreciate that you took so much time to acquaint me with the company. That care shown to a potential employee speaks well of your management style. It is no wonder the Campbell Soup Company retains its employees for so long. I feel I could learn a great deal from you and would certainly enjoy working with you.

In addition to my qualifications and experience, I will bring excellent work habits and judgment to this position. With the countless demands on your time, I am sure that you require people who can be trusted to carry out their responsibilities with minimal supervision. Given my range of experience and capacity to learn, I can readily undertake the additional duties that should result from the reorganization of the accounting department.

I look forward, Mr. Easterbrook, to hearing from you concerning your hiring decision. Again, thank you for your time and consideration.

Sincerely,

Karen Handelson

43 123rd Street
Bellerose, NY 11426
516-555-8652

Ms. Roberta Monet
AT&T
550 Madison Avenue
New York, NY 10022

Dear Ms. Monet,

I'd like to thank you for taking the time to talk with me Monday about the corporate adjuster position you have open at AT&T.

Your energetic presentation was enough to brighten anyone's Monday morning. I really appreciate that you took so much time to acquaint me with the company and its benefits. That care shown to a potential employee makes me feel I would be very comfortable working there.

I also enjoyed the challenging, thoughtful talk I had with Mr. Wilson. I felt a rapport and respect for him that I feel would facilitate a good working relationship.

I feel I have a good understanding of the requirements of the position, and I am very interested. I am even more confident than before of my ability to make a real contribution to AT&T.

Ms. Monet, thanks again for talking with me Monday. Should you or Mr. Wilson want to talk with me further, I would be more than happy to oblige. I look forward to the possibility of working with you.

Cordially,

Patricia Stevens

253 North 57th Avenue
Omaha, NE 68132
(402) 555-2029

May 4, 1994

Dr. Peter Newall
Director, University Relations
University of Nebraska-Omaha
Omaha, NE 68132

Dear Dr. Newall,

I'd like to thank you for taking the time to interview me for the staff writer position you have open.

I enjoyed meeting with you and am confident we could have an excellent working relationship.

Especially after meeting with you, I feel my background and expertise are a perfect fit for the job and its requirements.

Recapping my strengths and "fit" with the position:

• my previous short-term stints as staff writer with two suburban Lincoln colleges;

• my newspaper editing background would be an enormous asset because I have the inside track on what editors are looking for;

• my excellent "people skills" would enable me to fit into your congenial atmosphere as well as work well with the media and the university community.

I am also enclosing a piece I wrote expressing some of my ideas on how PR people could have more success getting their writing placed in the media.

Thank you again, Dr. Newall, for your time and consideration. I look forward to hearing from you around the first of the year.

Sincerely yours,

Carl Carlsburg

Recommended Reading

OBVIOUSLY, COVER LETTERS make up a small—albeit important—part of the job-search process. Here are some books that can fill in the gaps if you're unfamiliar with how to mount a major job search.

What Color is Your Parachute? (Richard Nelson Bolles, Ten Speed Press, $14.95.) The quintessential bible of job-hunting that, after almost twenty years, remains on lists of best-selling trade paperbacks and books most often checked out of libraries. This is not a detailed guide to resumes, cover letters, interviewing techniques, and so on. It's a more basic volume directed at those who aren't quite sure what they want to be when they grow up, and those who've decided they want a new career. Updated every year, *Parachute* is loaded with exercises that help the job-seeker or career-changer gain the self-knowledge needed to launch a successful job hunt. Bolles is not one to shy away from the more shocking statistics; he bombards the reader with reality because he wants to teach people how to tap the hidden job market. Enjoyable reading.

Who's Hiring Who (Richard Lathrop, Ten Speed Press, $9.95.) Something of a companion piece to *Parachute*. Bolles even calls it "the second best job-hunting guide on the market." Like Bolles, Lathrop emphasizes the hidden job market. Once you've read Bolles and know what you want to do, Lathrop will take you one step further, applying sharp marketing principles to resumes, cover letters, and interviews. Good information about interviewing, using contacts wisely, and getting maximum salary offers.

The Damn Good Resume Guide (Yana Parker, Ten Speed Press, $6.95.) A no-nonsense guide to resumes. Its format is extremely easy to follow, and it has many tips on creating effective resumes. It presents many samples of resumes and its companion volume, *The Resume Catalog* ($15.95), has even more.

The Overnight Resume (Donald Asher, Ten Speed Press, $7.95.) Asher, who makes his living writing resumes, packs a great deal into this concise volume, which is designed to jump-start a job search, especially the resume portion, quickly. He includes plenty of resume samples in a wide variety of styles and formats. Asher covers the resume-writing process step by step and includes additional advice on the job search. Another resume book by Asher, *From College to Career: Entry-Level Resumes for Any Major* (Ten Speed Press, $7.95), targets new graduates.

Put Your Degree to Work (Marcia R. Fox, Norton, $8.95.) Particularly directed at soon-to-be college graduates, especially in professional fields. Teaches one how to act like a professional, make the best use of college placement services, and the importance of having a mentor. Decent chapters on resumes and cover letters, but the book really shines in the interview chapter.

Real World 101 (Calano and Salzman, Warner, $3.95.) Works well as a companion to *Put Your Degree to Work*. While the latter deals in the specifics of the job search, *Real World 101* is more of a "head trip" book, designed to encourage students to adjust their attitudes to face life after college. The book spends relatively little time on job-hunting mechanics; it spends more time talking about how college has failed you, making the most of the college time you have left, and developing professional style. Has a useful chapter on goal-setting, as well as one on developing the reading, writing, and listening skills so essential for success in the business world.